Muddle Your Way Through Fatherhood

■ ■ ■

How to fool people into thinking you're a competent dad

By Paul Merrill

Text copyright © 2013 Paul Merrill
All Rights Reserved

This edition first published in 2013 by:

Thistle Publishing
36 Great Smith Street
London
SW1P 3BU

ISBN-13: 978-1-909609-46-4

Praise for *A Polar Bear Ate My Head* by Paul Merrill

"You're guaranteed a laugh a page."

The Observer

"Hilarious - and your boy will love it too!"

Cosmopolitan

"A bloody good lid-lifting expose. Frank, funny and enlightening. We have notified our lawyers. *****"

ZOO

"Memorable… rich comedy."

Bookseller & Publisher

"The best book ever written about the excesses and weirdness of the media. Every page is laugh-out-loud funny."

Will Storr

"I loved this book. So many incredible stories that I was laughing at nearly ever page. Just wonderful – hilarious, witty, but also very honest and touching."

Robert Salisbury, RNB Radio

"I loved it – a very good read."

Lisa Wilkinson, The Today Show

"Such a funny book - we loved it, and so did everyone in the office. You've really GOT to read it. "

WSFM Breakfast

"A Polar bear Ate My Head is a must read! Very funny - go buy it!"

Max Markson

"A very entertaining book. What he does well is deliver a fun read while still offering the research and business insights that go into launching and running a new magazine. Full of anecdotes and insider gossip. 9/10"

Encore Magazine

"This insider's look has the air of Toby Young's How to Lose Friends and Alienate People. *****"

The Weekly

"Enjoyable tales of misadventure in magazine land… he rises to the challenge with admirable gusto.*****"

Northern Weekly

"Straight up the funniest book I've ever read – and I haven't read many books."

Aussie Rules legend Warwick Capper

Available as a paperback or ebook from Amazon.com

Contents

Chapter 1: Should you become a dad   **1**
    Choosing the right mother   3
    Advantages/disadvantages of young mums/old mums   3
    Should you have kids quiz   5
    Adoption made easy   6

Chapter 2: Conception   **9**
    Is it better to have a boy or a girl?   10
    How to choose the sex of your baby   12
    Hermaphrodites: best of both worlds?   13
    Coping with crap sperm

Chapter 3: Pregnancy   **15**
    Sex during pregnancy   15
    Anti anti-natal classes   16
    Maternity wear   17
    Morning sickness: is it real?   17

Chapter 4: Birth   **20**
    The birth plan   20
    Home vs hospital   22
    The father's role
    Is it really that painful?
    Cutting the cord   27
    Things not to say

Chapter 5: Babies   **29**
    For the love of God why is it screaming?   30
    Choosing a name   33

How to change a nappy in 17 easy steps	35
Why won't the ungrateful brat even look at me?	37
Feeding and weaning	38
Why it's in your interest she breastfeeds	39
The nursery	40
A new dad's life in pie charts	41

Chapter 6: Toddlers 44

Toddler-proof your house	44
First words	45
Can we get someone else to look after it?	46
How to vet your babysitters	46
What if the babysitter is hot?	48
Nursery vs childminder – who does most damage?	48
Diary of a toddler holiday	49
Should you have another baby?	59
Advantages and disadvantages of only children	59
Kids who are close in age (fighters)	60
Kids who aren't (haters)	61
And how many should you have?	61

Chapter 7: School 64

The first day	64
Is your child a genius?	
…or as thick as shit?	65
Can you make your child smarter?	68
Bullying: all bad?	69
When your kid is being bullied	69
When your kid is the bully	71
Handy excuses for having a bully kid	73
What about girl bullies?	74
Homework	77
Surviving exams	78
Coping with failure	80
Not choosing bad subjects	82

Chapter 8: Help! They're getting bigger!   83
     Should you lie to your children?   84
     Good and bad lies explained   84
     How to tell perfect lies   86
     Mother's Day   87
     Father's Day   88
     Is your child depressed?   89
     7 tell-tale signs you have a depressed daughter   90
     7 tell-tale signs you have a depressed son   90
     How to ensure they're not nerds   91
     Is it better to bring up a serial killer or a nerd?   92
     Imaginary friends – good or bad?   94
     Are you ready to answer all their questions?   95
     Christmas   96
     How to prevent festive disasters   96
     Mistakes fathers make at Christmas   98
     Should you become a househusband?   99

Chapter 9: Teenagers   106
     How to tell if they are a teenager   107
     Teenage angst   109
     How to allay their fears   111
     Dad jokes   112
     Humour for different ages   114
     Are all other dads better than you?   115
     Fun ways to embarrass your teenager   118
     Internet grooming   120
     Are your kids taking drugs   120
     Clues that they might well be   122

Chapter 10: Birds and Bees   124
     What to include in your 'little talk'   125
     How to handle awkward questions   127
     10 ways to persuade your son not to become a father   128
     Is your child gay?   129

Their first boyfriend/girlfriend	130
Is he good enough for my daughter?	131
Is she good enough for my son?	133
Is your daughter a hooker?	134

Chapter 11: Adult children — **137**
- Is your child an adult? — 138
- Are they too stupid for college? — 139
- How to get them to move out — 141
- Surviving empty next syndrome — 142
- Is your daughter a terrorist? — 143
- Grandchildren — 144
- Are your children racist? — 145

Chapter 12: What can we learn from famous fathers? — **147**
- Ten best ever celebrity dad — 148
- Twelve worst ever celebrity dads — 152

Chapter 13: All your questions answered — **156**

Conclusion — **165**

Appendix I — **167**
- Fatherhood by numbers — 167

For my dad, who didn't need this book

1

Should YOU become a dad?

*Fatherhood is pretending the present you
love most is soap-on-a-rope.*
~ **Bill Cosby**

*To be a successful father, there's one absolute rule:
when you have a kid, don't look at it for the first two years.*
~ **Ernest Hemingway**

Congratulations! Just by picking this book up, you're already a 33% better dad! That number rises to 50% upon purchase.* Then, if you actually read it, your rating shoots up so far, you'll make your wife/girlfriend/lesbian egg donor look like a bad mum by comparison.

If you're bothering with this chapter, it's a good sign - it suggests that you're making an active choice about whether you would like children, weighing up options, making financial plans and assessing the appropriate multivitamins to conceive a genius.

Such a momentous decision will be informed by many factors, each of which will be considered scrupulously before you work out if now is the right time to begin trying to start a family.

* Disclaimer: Fatherhood skills may go up or down

This puts you in a better situation than those who skipped straight to Chapter 2 after a text from a casual shag, whose name they never knew, warned that she's a few days late and may have forgotten to take her pill the day of their brief union behind the bins in the McDonald's car park.

If that's you, don't panic! Yet. Well maybe panic a little, but then slap your own face and man up. This book will make allowances for your stupidity and will in no way make you feel patronised. You do understand what 'patronised' means, don't you? Good, you're a clever chap.

Read on, and I will arm you with all the vital information you need – not the boring guff you read about in parenting books.

And it's carefully tailored to you irrespective of whether you're a deadbeat already planning to fake your own death or a feckless chancer with a borstal of tattooed kids you've never met.

But let's assume for now that you've been more careful with the distribution of your seeds, and no gestation is taking place. Instead, you need to work out if the miracle of new life is for you or not. Because, as miracles go, it's not a cheap one.

The first thing to know is that the choice isn't yours, it's hers.

She will already have made the decision, probably chosen an appropriate month to conceive based on whether her mate, Shaz, told her it's better to have a Gemini or a Libran baby and chosen a name for both a boy and girl.

So really it's less of a decision making process and more about your negotiating skills. Even so, you still need to establish in your mind when *you* think the time is right so at least you have a starting position to begin bargaining from.

If, for example, she wants to get pregnant immediately, and you'd rather wait a couple of years, then you can compromise somewhere in the middle. And by 'middle' I mean at best a month or two away from *her* starting position.

But hang on, we're jumping ahead. The first thing to work out is if she is indeed The One. No point planting said seed in the wrong bed.

Choosing the right mum
She may be a sex-mad supermodel who loves football, beer and porn, with a rich, elderly father, but will she make a great mother?

And will you still be in love ten years down the track when the only modelling she's doing is for Argos, blow jobs are restricted to birthdays and her daddy left all his money to the family cat?

Are younger mums better than older ones?

Advantages of a young mum
- At least if you get an 18-year-old up the duff, the kids may have left school while you still have a bit of libido left.
- Like Will in The Inbetweeners, the child will benefit from the enhanced popularity that comes with a hot mum.
- Younger materials tend to resume their previous shape after stretching more than older cloth.
- More chance of you both being alive when the kid has finally grown to an age when he's making shitloads of money and can buy you a house
- You get to know your grandchildren for longer, and they can eventually help change your wife's colostomy bag for you in her dotage.

Advantages of an old mum
- More opportunities to reflect on wife's merits before you find yourself with four kids, a thirty-year mortgage and realise you married the wrong sister.

- If you become parents too soon, you have to watch all of your mates partying, drinking, playing the field and spending the summer in Ibiza. Club 18-30 doesn't have a kids' club or a children's menu.
- You don't live to see what little shits the grandchildren become.
- You've probably become too deaf to hear the baby screaming at night.

Of course, if you married a girl twenty years younger than you, then you can exploit the benefits of both - right up until she dumps you for one of your son's friends.

Also think about whether you want to get fatherhood out of the way quickly while you can still kick a football in the park, or whether it's better to wait a while until you've replaced the Vauxhall Nova with an Audi and can impress your kids' poorer friends.

For a quick reference, look at her mother, because that who you will be sleeping with in twenty five years. Hopefully, only in a figurative sense. If she's like Helen Mirren or Teri Hatcher, the odds favour you more than if she's more akin to Mollie Sugden or Kim Jong Il.

Either way, don't leave it too late and end up going down the Rod Stewart and Elton John route where your kids end up sticking you in a home while they're still in nappies.

Okay, let's assume you've chosen your life partner wisely, and made your best guess as to how she will perform as a mum.

Now the biggie: kids, or no kids? There's no middle option here. Except for a Tamagotchi.

You've bought this book, so make use of it. Take this scientific test and make sure you abide by the findings. Good luck!

And if you're flicking though this in the bookshop, for God's sake buy it. If you can't even commit to a book purchase, what sort of dad are you going to be anyway?

Is fatherhood for you?

This is a question not everyone asks of themselves. It is instead assumed by parents/girlfriends/friends/cell mates that one day you are bound to become a father. It's nature, innit? Why are we put on earth if not to sustain the species? Life's not all about fun, you know, it's about duty.

But that's dumb. You *do* have a choice. Think ahead a few years and imagine your life in two slightly different scenarios.

In one, you are carefree, wealthy and hedonistic. When you turn round to someone in the back seat of the car and ask them if them have their strap on, you're not talking about child restraints.

In the other, you see an older looking man with a resigned, stupefied expression hunched on a tiny wooden bench watching the fourth hour of the swimming gala waiting for the thirty seconds or so it'll take his overweight son to swim one width and be the only competitor requiring a float and arm bands.

Still undecided? OK, well try these questions…

1. On Sunday mornings do you like to:
a) Cuddle up with the missus, read the papers in bed with coffee and toast
b) Get woken at 5am by a screaming fight over the PS3 control, and find a dirty nappy left next to your pillow

2. Your ideal holiday is:
a) A couple of weeks in the Caribbean with a stack of good books to read by the pool sipping an ice cold local beer
b) A windswept fortnight in Bridlington sheltering from the rain inside a tent you got cheap from Aldi, playing Scrabble and eating wet rashers of burnt bacon.

3. You want your sex life to be:
a) Wild, animalistic and exciting
b) Formerly wild, animalistic and exciting

4. Weekends are for:
a) Long lie ins, catching up with friends, watching the footy, romantic meals, partying.
b) No lie ins, your kids being ferried to friends, watching a six-year-old play footy, Happy Meals and attending a party where everyone gets a slice of cake in a paper doily at the end.

5. You'd like your pride and joy to be:
a) A gleaming e-type Jag
b) A geeky looking kid on stage spitting pitifully into a trumpet attempting Twinkle Twinkle Little Star

6. In your later years, you'd like to:
a) Retire to a little cottage by the sea and travel the world
b) Retire to a little flat by the sewage works and be on 24-hour call for babysitting duties.

Mostly As

You're a selfish, lazy fool, and everyone hates you. But, wait! Before you take offence, realise that this wake up call has been the best thing that could have happened to you. Be thankful. Your life needs to move on to the next phase or else it will be meaningless and empty (though you will have more money, better holidays and a nice car). Procreate, impregnate and go forth and multiply. Then take offence.

Mostly Bs

You're either clinically too stupid to contemplate fatherhood, severely brain damaged or already have kids, in which case, why are you wasting time on a dumb quiz like this when you could be half way through Chapter 2 by now?

Should you adopt?

These days, it's very trendy to be seen about town with the latest designer pram accessorised with a little Ethiopian or Sudanese baby.

It shows you are charitable, altruistic, and possibly don't trust your wife's genes.

And don't worry - you don't need to risk disease and death-by-machete to actually go and pick one up, there are plenty of agencies that will be more than willing to do it for you. A few of them will actually deliver a baby in return for your life savings, while with others, the baby is mysteriously lost in the post.

Best plan is to send off your bank details to a helpful Nigerian who has offered to cut you in on his inheritance. At least he's in the same continent as the baby.

But adopting isn't easy. To be approved as potential adoptive parents, you must under go psychiatric tests, long, invasive interrogations, police checks, full medicals and meet strict age and weight criteria. You will be grilled on your religion, attitude to homosexuality, how many green vegetables you consume and whether your house complies with the European Union's Health and Safety legislation.

All this while the 17-year-old chain-smoking drug dealer next door is having her fourth kid by four different prisoners and giving them matching nose piercings.

Advantages and disadvantages

Advantages
- Savings on maternity wear
- Some come already house trained
- Wife's body has no 'Out of action' period.
- The kid comes with a full service history

Disadvantages
- Most don't come with a 30-day trial or money back plan
- Awkward conversation if they discover their real parents were a serial killing brother and sister or, worse, Welsh.
- Awkward conversation if they discover their real parents are billionaire philanthropists or, better still, Posh and Becks.
- Have you read the Midwich Cuckoos?

So, you've made your mind up, and hopefully decided to become a dad.

Well done.

There is, however, still time to reconsider. No? Okay then, you're really going to go ahead. Afterall, bringing up a kid these days only costs about £200,000, and what would you need all that cash for? It'd only be frittered away on a bigger house, sports car, booze and partying. And you're going to leave all those things behind, aren't you?

As I said, no point in rushing things. If there are any doubts, simply read this chapter again, and then again. If you're still certain, I guess you're ready to turn the page. Unless you think you might change your mind. Did I mention it's not too late?

2

Conception

Never raise your hand to your kids. It leaves your groin unprotected.
~ Red Buttons

"If evolution really works, how come mothers only have two hands?"
~ Milton Berle

In theory, this is the only part of fatherhood which is a) guaranteed to be fun, and b) doesn't require any practice or prior knowledge.

Ha! As if. To a woman, sex may be a leisure pursuit, but when she's in full conception mode, it is a cynical operation devoid of passion where failure of any kind will be traced back to your shortcomings.

Kids are conceived in two ways:
a) Miracles from God. This means a terrible accident involving a split condom or a devious spouse. Or both. As her biological clock ticks, so 'accidents' have to be planned as thoroughly as the casino heist in Ocean's Eleven.
b) Miracles from science. If a woman takes longer than two months to conceive, then panic will set in. Her friends will tell her it's all down to the lunar cycle and which herbal tea she drinks before bed, her mother will chip in that infertility goes

back generations in her family and that maybe she should give up, and you'll reassure her that these things take time and there's no need to worry.

Of all of these opinions, yours will be dismissed as completely ludicrous, and more proof that you're clearly not taking it seriously enough.

From that moment on, masturbation and casual love making are banned and an app on her smartphone will flash at the precise moment you need to be shooting your load directly into her uterus. Forgot foreplay, or snuggling up in each other's arms afterwards, seconds count. The moment you're done, like a praying mantis, you'll be dispatched so that she can get her pelvis into a forty-five degree angle to help your plainly inadequate sperm bumble their way haplessly towards the egg.

Just as you struggled to get your 10m swimming badge so your little swimmers may be facing an uphill battle. And if you've ever tried to swim uphill, you'll know what they're up against*.

If the process doesn't work, you'll find yourself at a clinic the next day with your wife asking a physician to test your semen for any signs of life and berating you openly for not eating enough zinc.

Is it better to have a boy or a girl?

One of God's meanest acts was to leave the sex of your child down to chance. So this section is only actually useful if you're in Mogadishu deciding which malnourished infant to take home with you.

Otherwise, even if you can't affect the outcome, at least you've been warned.

* Gravity

Advantages of boys
1. You don't have to pay for weddings, abortions and sanitary products.
2. There's a chance they'll bring home a sexy girlfriend who'll be impressed with your BMW
3. Wet dreams are easier to shift from sheets than that first period.
4. Going to the skate park is marginally better than an hour braiding Malibu Barbie's hair.
5. Once they reach eight, you can justify taking them to Transformers 9 or Fast and Furious 17 on the pretence that it's for them not you. With girls, they go straight from The Fairy Princess to anything starring Jennifer Aniston and will cry in all films more scary than Alvin and the Chipmunks.
6. You avoid the emasculating prospect that a daughter will bring home a handsome boyfriend who is everything you're not.
7. Your grandchildren get to keep your surname, so no risk of them being called Hardcock, Smellie or Lardbottom.

Advantages of girls
1. Fewer broken windows, broken toys and broken kids next door
2. In the event of your daughter bringing home a sexy girl, there is a clear dilemma as to who pays for wedding. If you suspect your daughter is the 'man' of the relationship, assure the other parents that they need to pay. As a gesture, you'll chip in to hiring a tux for your daughter.
3. You don't have to have the embarrassing birds and bees talk.
4. Extra help for your wife in the kitchen (though best don't quote that one to her).
5. Finding out that your 15-year-old daughter is pregnant isn't great, but it's less traumatic than a Neanderthal with an

Everton tatt turning up with a shotgun accusing your 15-year-old son of impregnating his daughter.

So, there it is, scientifically proven - more reasons to have a boy. Maybe the Chinese got it right after all.

However, there are enough crackpots (and, possibly, serious scientists) out there who reckon you *can* choose the gender of your baby. I bet now you wish you'd read this *before* you have your eleventh baby girl, eh?
So, if the idea of having one particular sex terrifies you, then there is hope after all and less need to deposit the baby on some church steps. In your face, God! Now we just need to work on isolating that red hair gene.

If you want a boy...
1. **No wanking!** (Not even in secret).
    According to Dr Laudram Shettles, from Columbia University, to get a boy, the father must not ejaculate for five days before the attempt.
2. **Set your watch**
    Surveys have found that the perfect time to have sex is precisely twelve hours before ovulation. A minute either way, and you may as well wait another month.
3. **No double dips**
    Once you've finished, roll over and go to sleep. Apparently doing it again makes a girl more likely if sperm on the way to the egg are persuaded to retreat by a second group headed the other way.
4. **Monitor her mucus at all costs**
    The eminent Dr Shettles also claims that your odds will favour a boy if you time your session 'as close as possible to the shift from peak mucus back to thicker, cloudier mucus'.

And nothing is going to bring on your moment of ecstasy faster than when she cries out: 'For fuck's sake cum, I can feel my mucus clouding over!'

If you want a girl…
1. **Be a bad lover**

    If a woman orgasms, then she's more likely to have a boy. So go easy with that thing you do. Talk about football, or do all those things she says she hates. If she's still getting too excited, give her a copy of Women's Weekly to read while you get on with it.

2. **Have pitiful sperm**

    A low sperm count means you're more likely to conceive a girl. Actually, it means you're more likely to not have anything, but if one of the little fellas does make it, he'll see to it that no penis is attached to the foetus.

3. **Pour in lashings of vinegar.**

    If you've produced eight sons, but no daughter, it could be that your wife's vagina isn't acidic enough (unlike her tongue). So if it doesn't taste of lemon juice or battery acid, it's too alkaline. Just make sure you save enough for your chips.

4. **Go missionary**

    For some reason, more girls are produced when couples use the missionary position. If you're not aware of any other positions, and want a boy, you're in trouble.

Hermaphrodites: best of both worlds?

I'm sure we've all harboured a secret desire to have both external *and* internal genitalia at one time or another.

If it's good enough for snails, molluscs and jellyfish, then why not us? The advantages are all too obvious:
1. Choice of male or female toilet
2. Ability to give birth *and* open jars

3. Potential for a great party trick
4. Chance to get yourself pregnant.

Ok, so there may be the odd awkward social interaction for them, but as their parent, you can simultaneously plait their beautiful silk-like hair and take them to the park for a kick around. And slugs don't seem to have many issues being a part of the transgender community.

However, if you've set your heart on having one, there are steps you can take:

1. See a shrink
2. If you're still so inclined, get money back from first shrink and see another
3. Do all of the above then have sex with Jamie Lee Curtis or Lady Gaga.

3

Pregnancy

My father had a profound influence on me. He was a lunatic.
~ Spike Milligan

Birth is the beginning of death
~ Thomas Fuller (17th century writer)

Most women claim to 'know' they are pregnant before confirming it with a kit from Boots. That said, it's still not worth asking them why, if they knew already, they still had to buy five testers at £15 each. Also don't suggest sarcastically that the white plastic devices with their tell-tale blue lines could be arranged in a frame and called 'Piss artist'.

Pregnancy brings with it several potentially troubling situations for the father, all of which need to be dealt with carefully. The overriding rule is to apologise, even if you're not sure what you're apologising for, or you're certain that you are in the right.
Because you're not in the right, even if you are.

Sex during pregnancy

During the first trimester, this will involve the fragrant taste of vomit when kissing, and, by the final trimester, kisses are trickier as you'll be doing it doggie style.

Remember that the woman will feel physically sick early on (not just at your naked body this time), but once she reaches three months, she'll be a sex-crazed psycho until she gets towards full term when the 'sex-crazed' bit of 'sex-crazed psycho' can be deleted.

Added vaginal swelling means she'll be hot for you at the same time as being exhausted and resentful that it was you who made her pregnant. This can result in some passionate sex with an angry, violent undercurrent.

Antenatal classes

These begin at the latter stages of pregnancy and are supposed to teach you everything about becoming a parent. They involve six couples sitting in a circle being spoken down to by a large, dishevelled lady clutching a working model of a woman's reproductive system in one hand and a breast pump in the other.

Her primary mission is to scare the shit out of both of you for an hour, and make you, the father-to-be, specifically feel inadequate.

The mothers-to-be eagerly ask about pelvic floor muscles, birth plans and mobile epidurals while the dads squirm every time someone mentions afterbirth or perineum.

Then, the moderator will lead the entire room in a series of stress-relieving yoga positions while you and the other dads exchange awkward glances.

The three golden rules for these classes are:

1. Don't ask her when it's safe to have sex again. For this woman, sex is a necessary evil and used wholly for reproductive purposes.
2. An energy drink taken seconds before entering the room can prevent you falling asleep. If you do nod off, just explain that you were experimenting with relaxation techniques.
3. Do not suggest that you have ever felt pain worse than childbirth, especially if you actually have. Never stray from the hymn sheet that states that childbirth is the single worst pain any human being has ever been subjected to, including

ancient Chinese tortures. This is covered in more depth in the next chapter.

The bump

A woman's pregnancy bump, while a wondrous thing to behold, also has its dangers. If her 'eating for two' regime has involved eating for two water buffalos then there's a chance it isn't as neat as she might have wanted. However, your job is to make her feel that whatever unusual shape she has morphed into, it is the single most beautiful thing you've ever seen.

The inevitable question: 'Does my body disgust you?' has a right and a wrong answer:

Wrong answer 1: 'Don't worry, love, it's not for much longer.'

Wrong answer 2: 'Disgust is a strong word…'

Correct answer: 'No, my sweet darling, pregnancy suits you.'

There is no need to add: '…although attending step aerobics classes thrice weekly directly after the birth will also suit you' or 'Didn't Posh do well to get her figure back within eight days?'

A pair of decent women's jeans may cost £40 or so. The same pair with an elastic pouch crudely stitched into the front suddenly becomes £900. And, no, apparently they can't just hang their stomach over their trousers like you do. Can't, or won't?

Either way, maternity clothes cost more per kilogram than gold bullion, so get her to sign a contract stating that she promises to breast feed for the first five years so at least you save on formula milk, and also don't have to walk to the corner shop in the rain if you need a drop for your tea.

Morning sickness

Waking up to a desperate compulsion to vomit is nothing new to the average man. But to a woman, it's a new, wonderful part of having a foetus growing inside. You'd think something so natural would be accepted, but no.

Morning sickness will rear its ugly head for the first three months of the pregnancy. In fact, your wife will rear her (hopefully not ugly) face in front of the toilet seconds after she wakes up, like a bulimic who's dreamed of eating pie.

Mentioning your hangover won't illicit much sympathy, especially if you imply it deserves equal sympathy. Instead, try these tips to survive these tricky few weeks.

1. Forget rolling on top of her first thing expecting a quickie. It's a mistake you'll only make once.
2. Reassure her that the pain she'll feel later on in the pregnancy will be much worse.
3. If she can't face eating anything, suggest she makes you a full English to see if it helps with her appetite.
4. Tell her you're still available for that quickie, if she doesn't mind swilling some mouthwash first.

Eating for two

Even at full term, a pregnant woman only needs to eat the calorific equivalent of an extra Mars Bar a day. Which means you've probably been effectively eating for two since puberty.

Nevertheless, you will be blamed if: a) you suggest she's overeating, or b) you don't suggest it and she piles on impossible-to-shift weight.

Best plan is to present her with a free gym membership and Weight Watchers vouchers the moment she sprogs as a thank you for giving you a child.

If she's sedated enough, there's a slim chance they won't get shoved into one of your orifices.

Buying baby clothes

Under no circumstances make the schoolboy error of buying any baby clothes beyond the cheapest babygros from Tesco. Anything else is a waste of money. And never forget that your days of actually owning money are about to be extinguished forever.

If you think this is an exaggeration, look at the price of baby shoes. Despite the fact they are made from about three square inches of leather, which could easily have been harvested from a dormouse, they cost more than the pair of Doc Martens you bought last year.

You'll be given baby clothes from three main sources:

1. Rich friends will inevitably buy a Little Lord Fauntleroy outfit consisting of a linen, hand-embroidered, hand smocked Peter Pan collared shirt, velvet pantaloons and a cashmere tam-o-shanter. All dry clean only.
2. Your best mate will buy the baby an 'amusing' babygro with a slogan immediately deemed 'inappropriate' by your wife.
3. Grandmothers will knit a hideous 50s-style chunky wool jumper with the baby's initials lovingly stitched in.

All of the above clothes will be put on baby, remain in place for between thirty seconds and a minute before being drenched in vomit, piss or milk. Baby will then be stripped off and redressed in the baby-gros you bought for 50p each.

The outfits will never be worn again.

The birth

*"On the one hand, we'll never experience childbirth.
On the other hand, we can open all our own jars."*
~ Bruce Willis

*"Childbirth is a miracle. No, it's not. . . . It's
a chemical reaction, that's all"*
~ Bill Hicks

The birth plan

Back in the day, a birth plan involved the husband chucking the wife and a change of clothes in the back of the Ford Cortina, dropping them at the hospital and then going to work.

Job done.

A few hours later, he would be phoned by a nurse and invited to meet his new child who had been washed, dressed and wrapped up. His wife would have had time to be fully cleaned, sedated and tucked up in bed so the three of them could bathe in the glow of love and new life until another nurse came, took the kid and the father could go home to watch Match of The Day while his mother cooked him a steak and kidney pie.

These days, a birth plan can make the St James Bible look like a leaflet. Every second of the few hours between waters breaking and baby emerging must be accounted for and planned with a level of meticulous detail akin to a space shuttle launch.

Your involvement in the drawing up of the plan will be minimal, apart from being asked the odd question such as whether a Peruvian nose flautist or Adele would be more relaxing and whether the essential oil burner should contain bergamot or ylang ylang.

If your answer contains the words 'Status Quo's Greatest Hits' or 'a Glade Pine Forest air freshener' you will not be consulted again.

In the plan, you will be referred to as a 'birth companion' throughout.

Elsewhere will be a list of phone numbers to call to announce the new arrival (and woe betide the man who calls *his* mother before *her* mother) and the desired form of pain relief.

Unless you are a devoted Scientologist, don't be tempted to say that surely gas and air will suffice. In fact, even if you are an L Ron Hubbard fan, this may be a good time to depart momentarily from his teachings as no man should stray within eye-gouging distance from a woman in the throes of extreme labour pain whose husband turned down the epidural on her behalf.

The next thing she will ponder is the birthing position. Again, you can sit this little debate out, however…

If you want to sound caring say: If you lie down the contractions will be stronger and it'll narrow the passage through the cervix.

If you don't want to sound caring say: I always thought you only knew one position anyway.

By far the most important part of the plan, however, is where exactly the ordeal will take place. Assuming you don't live near a forest clearing where woodland animals will gather to see the miracle of the new baby's birth to the sound of songbirds and unicorns braying their approval, then you'll need to decide whether she wants a hospital birth, or a home one.

This, as you'll see, is a decision you don't want to get wrong…

Home birth horrors

Firstly, don't let anyone tell you that it's even worth considering having the kid in your sitting room. It's not. But your wife will have had her more hippyish friends chewing off her ear about how wonderful, life affirming and serene it is and how hospitals are evil breeding grounds for superbugs.

The father's job in all of this is to do everything humanly possible to put her off.

First use gentle persuasion, then emotional blackmail, and if all that fails, cut out and give her this entirely fictional list of 'facts' about home birth babies:

1. Babies born in the home scream an average of three hours more per day
2. Home birth kids get parole six months later than those born in a hospital
3. Girls not born in a delivery suite will be short of five essential enzymes and will become allergic to Jersey Shore.
4. Mothers who refuse a hospital birth get 27.4% more stretch marks, require 6.7 more stiches and are 43.9% less likely to have a prolapsed colon.

Source: Schwarzkov, Sielmann and Garrolding, British Medical Journal 2010

The real reasons for avoiding home births are just as compelling, as this genuine* and moving diary written by a father will testify...

Diary of a home birth
Thursday Feb 12th

Just a week to go now. Letitia is blooming and the house is nearly ready for our arrival. I feel so blessed. Just a few last minute things to

* Incident described may not actually be genuine

buy to make the experience as special as possible. I'm so glad Letitia talked me into a home birth.

Friday Feb 13th

Letitia's mum popped round with a lovely knitted cardigan and a bobble hat. So sweet of her. I've also downloaded the Enya album that Letitia wants to be playing as the baby's head appears and ordered the rose otto oil, as they didn't have any at Boots. I have a folded pile of freshly ironed Egyptian cotton white towels, I've charged the camera and the handycam and cleared a space in the sitting room for the birthing pool. If I do say so myself, I am feeling rather smug! There's nothing like being prepared.

Sunday Feb 15th

Letitia had a few contractions today, but thankfully it was a false alarm! I mean, the baby can hardly arrive before I have the 'soft fluorescence' light bulbs put in and had the room feng shuied, can it???

Even Bertie, our shitsu is excited!

Monday Feb 16th

The Feng Shui expert we had recommended by Letitia's BFF, Portia, visited us today. Mr Dhapsar kindly assessed the house and said that I had to move the telly to the other side of the room to channel the energy lines, put a pot plant by the stairs and make the sitting room door open to the left instead of the right. I laughed and told Letitia that we could hardly take the door off its hinges and rewire the entire room just to reposition the TV!! But she felt that that was exactly what needed to be done. She was also cross that I hadn't thought of it before.

Tuesday Feb 17th

The pool has arrived! It's a bit bigger than I thought, so I had to lug the sofa into the kitchen and take down the shelves I put up last week, but that's OK. I've also got the door off it hinges, and cut a hole in the plaster by the bay window so I can move the TV before the big day. Apparently the warm water will take away most of the pain of childbirth.

Wednesday Feb 18th
 4am More contractions. It's still too soon. I've sent her back to bed with her favourite dandelion root tea
 4.15am Her waters have broken all over the duck down quilt. Contractions getting stronger. Left Letitia in bed and spent 15 minutes searching the garage for the electric pump to get the pool up. I've also put on a few saucepans to get some hot water.
 4.25am Phoned the midwife, but she's helping another lady give birth apparently. They're going to send a replacement called Serge round. Letitia wants me to phone the dry cleaners about the quilt, but I pointed out it's a bit early. Still no sign of the blessed pump.
 4.32am Managed to find a foot pump, and started to inflate the ruddy thing. Contractions very intense. Letitia screaming in agony with each one and demanding pain relief. I smiled and pointed out that she had opted for no pain relief, but this didn't help.
 4.41am The pool's about half up. Still no sign of Serge. I lit an oil burner as the room was a bit smelly for some reason, but, as the rose otto hadn't arrived yet, I tried scooping out the cartridge from the Glade plug in instead. The water on the stove was boiling, so poured it into the pool and put some more pans on.
 4.55am Finally Serge is here. I think he's Hungarian, or maybe Austrian. Lovely chap, but doesn't speak a word of English. Found out the smell was Bertie. He'd been rolling around on the dirty quilt and was soaking wet.
 5.59am The pool is finally inflated. My leg feels like it's going to fall off, but still excited by what's about to happen. Serge made me move the door I'd taken off its hinges so that he could set out some towels.

6.02am The pool's pretty full now. It's a bit chilly despite all my pans. I helped Letitia in and (silly me!) I'd filled it too high so a wave of water drenched the carpet and all the baby clothes I'd laid out. Serge shook his head slowly and indicated that I'd need to get some more out.

6.06am I think the baby's coming! Letitia screamed louder than I'd ever heard her before. I told her that we were nearly there, but she pointed down at the side of the pool where a stream of water was gushing out. I think her bracelet must have caught it.

6.09am The only other baby clothes we had are a cute Halloween pumpkin costume for a one-year-old. I'm sure it'll be fine. I managed to set up the handycam on a tripod just as the next contraction occurred and unfortunately Letitia knocked it off into the pool. The water spreading over the Axminster is now a murky browny red colour. I've bailed some of it back in, but the Band Aid I put over the hole hasn't really worked.

6.10am Letitia got quite agitated that there was no music. I found my ipod, but it turns out I'd got the wrong Enya album. Who knew there was more than one? I tried with one hand to access iTunes and use the other to point the camera, but Letitia seemed to think it was too soon for photos.

6.11 Bertie started drinking the water on the carpet, so I pushed him to one side and dropped the ipod into the slush. Bertie's claw must have scratched the side of the pool and we all heard a loud pop. Serge said something that sounded urgent and Letitia gave a mighty yell. I realised the baby was coming out.

Used one hand to try to stop the air coming out of the first hole and the other to cover the new one. Using my chin, I pressed play on the CD which was in our stereo. Turned out to be Meatloaf.

6.13am Serge was speaking into his mobile. Apparently the baby's 'breached' which sounds a bit like what happens to a whale. I was about to point this out to Letitia when there was a loud crack, all the lights went out and Bat out of Hell suddenly stopped midway through. It was still pitch black outside so I tried to light a match but they were too damp. There was a terrible electric burning smell coming from where I was about to install the TV.

6.14am Had to abandon attempts to keep the pool inflated. Most of the water has poured out anyway, so Letitia was left with her bottom half still wedged inside the rubber, and the rest of her sprawled rather unfortunately on the carpet. Now she really does look beached.

6.16am Frantic knocking at the door. The ambulance has arrived. They refused an offer of tea and instead said that they had to get her out asap. They put her on the door I'd taken down to give her support, but unfortunately she wouldn't fit through the doorway. One of the ambulancemen got out an axe (I didn't even know they carried them!) and managed to hack off the entire bay window. She was lifted through and they carried her through the flowerbeds into the ambulance.

7.23am Our beautiful daughter, Hope, has been born. Letitia seems calmer, but has told me that it was all my fault for not persuading her to have it in a hospital in the first place and that the house had better be perfect by the time she comes home tomorrow morning.

How to avoid pain during childbirth
(yours, not hers)

Do say: Just focus on your breathing, and lean on my shoulder when the next contraction comes.
Don't say: I wonder if Utd are still winning

Do say: Ok, short, sharp breaths, the epidural will take effect very soon.
Don't say: I'm sure it's not worse than when I sprained my ankle on the Norfolk Broads.

Do say: Oh wow, I can see the baby's head!
Don't say: Holy fuck, what is that thing? Aagh, it's like a piece of gristle!

Do say: I'm here every second of the way, Babe.
Don't say: I've told the doctor not to revive you if you stop breathing.

Do say: OK, love one more big push. You can do it!
Don't say: Jeez, love, have you followed through?

Do say: You did great, my darling. I'm so proud
Don't say: See, I told you it would be a piece of cake

Cutting the cord

After the baby's out, you will be asked by the midwife if you'd like to cut the cord. A pair of scissors will be presented along with a thick, fibrous, blood-coated piece of tubing that looks the same as the one that connected the alien to John Hurt's stomach.

Only the alien life form it's attached to is louder, but probably more dangerous.

This duty is either the single most beautiful, meaningful task you'll ever perform, or, for the other 99.999% of men, too horrendous, unnatural and grisly to even consider

So, to avoid having to conjure up an excuse on your feet, just pluck one from this list.

1. Sorry, would love to, but the terms of my parole mean I can't handle sharp objects.
2. Are they left handed scissors? No? What a shame.
3. (violently shake your right hand up and down) Damn Parkinson's!
4. I'd like *you* to perform this sacred procedure while I recite a short Buddhist prayer.
5. Thank you, but I'd rather lick my way to the centre of the Earth, and, anyway, you're the professional so you cut the bloody thing while I look the other way.

Any suggestion that you might want to follow the tradition of taking the afterbirth and placenta home to bury in the garden or even to cook up for dinner can be safely met with nervous laughter, or by fainting.

So, you've somehow survived the birth and now have a real life baby to gently cradle while your wife is hosed down, stitched and fumigated behind you. Congratulations, you have cleared the first hurdle.

Soon, there will be a realisation that this thing is here for good; that you are at least partly responsible for it. This can be a terrifying thought. I mean, what do you know about taking responsibility?

So, while manoeuvring the baby (which, by the way, you should avoid calling 'it') into the crook of your arm, turn the page and read about the wonderful*, precious days ahead.

* Warning: this sentence was included to boost your hope and morale. Days ahead may not be wonderful. Who are we kidding – they will at times be a living hell, so just don't read this disclaimer

5

Babies

When a baby comes you can smell two things: the smell of flesh, which smells like chicken soup, and the smell of lilies, the flower of another garden, the spiritual garden.
~ Carlos Santana

"Spread the diaper in the position of the diamond with you at bat. Then, fold second base down to home and set the baby on the pitcher's mound. Put first base and third together, bring up home plate and pin the three together. Of course, in case of rain, you gotta call the game and start all over again."
~ Jimmy Piersall

Phew! So, you've given birth (as near as dammit), got the thing home, have a mantelpiece full of cards congratulating you and your wife has recovered from the delivery enough to be able to resume house-care duties.

However, in the frenzied lead up to the birth, it somehow slipped your mind that you will have to look after it *forever*.

Starting right now.

The first thing you'll realise is that babies are very unreasonable people. In fact they are greedy, ungrateful, pudgy and hell-bent on getting their own way. Think Alan Sugar, but with less hate.

And, just like Alan, all they will scream, vomit, sleep, scream some more and drink milk.

The second thing to take on board is that babies are not a full time job. Oh no. A full time job s nine until five with an hour for lunch and weekends free. Babies are three full time jobs at once. And you'll wish *you* had three actual full time jobs to escape their evil demands.

You can patiently explain to a newborn that nights are for sleeping, and that Daddy has been invited out by his mates to wet the baby's head, but they stubbornly refuse to accept it.

So, first things first. The most pressing issue is the scream.

For the love of God, why is it screaming?
...and please make it stop

About twelve of your sixteen or so waking hours will be filled with ear drum-piercing crying and wailing. Of the remaining eight hours, three will involve more screaming, two will be spent rocking the baby back to sleep, one will be frantically sterilising bottles and dummies, and during the other two, you'll be in a fitful zombie-like state wondering why there's no crying and whether you need to check whether it's still breathing.

Babies scream if they are too hot, too cold, hungry, overfed, full of wind, are teething, in severe pain, bored, scared of the dark and just because they want attention.

From Day One, your wife will be able to instinctively diagnose the reason for the outburst, and you will be expected to learn. Trying to force milk down the throat of an already full baby or lovingly putting extra blankets over a child with a temperature of 108 might not get the results you're looking for.

So next time the little mite is trying to blow the speaker on the baby monitor, make sure you have this handy flowchart to hand*...

* It's quite possible that this hasn't been wholly verified by any pediatrician, professional healthcare body, or indeed anyone.

Is the baby screaming?
No - Then why are you reading this?
Yes – Continue to next question

Is it red in the face?
No - Really? Are you in a freezing tundra then?
Yes - Ok, don't panic - Continue

Have you fed it in the last 24 hours?
No - Dial 999 and hand yourself in.
Yes - Continue

Does it look in pain?
No – Wait… yes it does a bit - Continue
Yes - Continue

Did you wind it after its last feed?
No - Tilt baby at various angles until you feel a large escape of air (from the baby). If there was also a large escape of vomit, change your shirt.
Yes - Continue

Is your wife standing nearby?
No - Continue
Yes – wander within earshot, look helpless

Try singing - Continue

Now try singing something more suitable for kids – Continue

Are you sitting down?
Yes - Well stand up and jiggle a bit, you lazy sod - Continue
No – Jiggle anyway - Continue

Does it feel a bit cold?
 No – continue
 Yes – **Well, are you standing outside in the rain?**
  - Why, yes, I am – Proceed inside, your wife was right about you – back to top of flowchart
  - No – Stop jiggling and wrap it in the nearest blanket you can find (not the dog's)

Is it bright red, sweating like Chaz Bono and as warm as a hot water bottle?
 Yes – Consider taking off clothes. – No no, the baby's clothes
 No - Continue

Did you let it watch Schindler's List?
 Yes – You idiot, try it with something less traumatic like Beaches, but skip the ending
 No - Continue

Are you standing on its foot?
 Wait, yes, I am – Stop standing on its foot
 No – Continue

Jeez, is it still screaming
 No, it's fallen asleep – place in cot, then run
 Yes – Really? Well, just jiggle a while longer until help arrives

I hope you're now reassured that whatever the reason for the scream, there is a solution. Unfortunately the solution won't always stop the screaming as soon it will learn that all it has to do is cry loudly and it'll get picked up, fed, made warmer or jiggled.

Also, you've got to stop calling it 'it'. It has a name, doesn't it? No? OK, then maybe that's the next thing to think about.

Choosing a name

This should be a simple enough task, but is made less simple by baby name books containing 16,000 possible choices, and a hormonal pregnant wife not thinking rationally.

The ideal name is unusual enough that there won't be seven others in his or her class, but not so weird that you can't find it on a key fob in a tacky souvenir shop.

Remember, a St John, Tarquin or Xavier won't last long in parts of Wolverhampton, and a Derek, Bernard or Albert might not thank you when they become emos.

Flower, Petal, River and Blossom will (rightfully) be bullied to within an inch of their lives while John, Robert, Jane and Keith are destined to work in book keeping and play online role playing games for hours in a darkened room.

A family name is a nice idea, but fraught with problems if the immediate choices are Reginald, Ethel and Evadne. You may need to go back a generation or three in search of alternatives. If this still proves fruitless, ask if any of them had a dog.

Also think about how the name will fit with your surname. A few examples of ill-advised choices might be:

Chris Peacock	Dick N Cider
Mike Litoris	Wayne Kerr
Hugh Jass	Anna Linjection
Mike Hunt	Phil McKaffety
Pat McRotch	Betty Bangzer
Courtney Fish	Keith Chegwin

A cute little bubba wrapped in soft blankets might suit Poppet or Pixyboo, but try to imagine her forty years later as an obese single mum of eight in polka dot leggings selling crack and turning tricks for clean needles.

Equally, if you've cleverly combined the names of you and your wife to create something hideous like Lilyeric or 'Sharonalf, then it's unlikely she'll become a captain of industry or prime minister any time soon.

And if you've always wanted to name your first born son after one of your sporting heroes, never admit this to your wife. Instead, tell her that the name belonged to a much-loved uncle who died heroically for his country, saving many lives in the process, having previously developed a cure for a virulent form of breast cancer. That way, you've got half a chance of getting 'Wayne' or 'Bradley' past her, but don't push it by mentioning another gallant relative called 'Rooney' or 'Wiggins'. She'll also eventually realise that your suggestion of the traditional Native American name Eisrepvan is Van Persie backwards.

One thing to be aware of is a sneaky trick employed by some women to make you like their ridiculous choice of name. In the following exchange, the woman has her heart set on calling her baby son Kit, a name her husband hates…

Wife: Hi Bill, there's something very special I'd like to share with you. Something very important to me.
Husband: OK, sure. Fire away
Wife: Well, I've decided that I would like to call our son after my great uncle because he meant so much. He was practically a father to me. Mum cried with joy when I told her.
Husband: You already told your mum? OK. Well, he sounds a good man. What was his name?
Wife: Godfrey
Husband: Godfrey?
Wife: Yes, it's such a sweet name. Maybe he could be Goddy for short.
Husband: Er, look, I know how much he meant, but I really don't think that…

Wife (crying): He was a war hero, lost his leg in Burma saving his battalion from the Japanese. If our son could be half the man he was…

Husband: I know, Honey, but Godfrey? Don't you think it's a little…old?

Wife (Now hysterical): Oh Bill, please, I'm begging you to support me in this. This means too much to my family. I'm afraid I can't call him any other name. This is just too important.

Husband: Well, look, er, I don't want to… but, love, I can't call him Godfrey. He'd be teased at school. And I thought we'd agreed on Daniel.

Wife: (still weeping): Oh God, I don't want to go on if we can't remember Uncle Godfrey. Mum will be inconsolable if we change out minds now.

Husband: Change our… but we never… look, my darling, I'd do anything to make your happy, but I don't think Godfrey is… Did he have a middle name or something?

Wife: Yes, but you'll hate that too. I'm calling him Godfrey because I love my country.

Husband? What was the middle name then?

Wife: (now dabbing tears away) Kit

Husband: Oh, I see. Well, I suppose it's not so terrible. I mean, I really like Dan, but if it means this much to you, then Kit's OK.

You see how manipulative they can be if you're not on your toes. You could always pre-empt her by using these tactics yourself and suggesting names like Gertrude, Ethel, Reginald, Percy, Rodney or Elton, but don't do it at the same time as there will be too many tears.

How to change a nappy in 17 easy steps

This is something the modern father will attempt an average of 827 times per child. That number may have been made up, but the actual total will be a big one, so you're going to need to know what to do. Pin these instructions up in the nursery…

1. Establish if the nappy is indeed in need of changing. Do this by looking for the tell tale brown smudge on your white carpet or by copping a putrid whiff of something ungodly.
2. See if anyone else is available to perform the change. If they are, subtly position the baby so the smell will waft to that person and then disappear for a few minutes.
Having had the child dumped back in your hands by unimpressed wife, proceed to the change mat.
3. Place baby on change mat
4. No, face up.
5. Remove old nappy, and attempt to place in nappy sack. After rolling the sack between your fingers, trying to get it to open, start ripping violently at it in frustration.
6. Find another nappy sack, open and place the stinking nappy inside.
7. Gently clean the baby's bits with a series of moist wipes, then curse inwardly that you've already tied up the nappy sack.
8. Find another nappy sack and attempt to open.
9. After baby is clean, tie nappy sack and position the new nappy under its bottom.
    This is the moment the adorable little thing will choose to piss everywhere. For boys it will be a jet into your eye; for girls, a pool will form and then drip down your trousers.
10. Get several more wipes to stem the flow, grab another nappy sack and force the newly soaked nappy and all the wipes inside.
11. Get another nappy in position, pull up those side tags things and press them down on the baby's tummy.
12. Wipe brow (unless hand covered in faeces).

13. Find that the drawer containing the clean babygros is just out of reach. Wonder for a few seconds the chances of the baby rolling off the change table during the three seconds you'll need to retrieve the garment.
14. Pick up baby, open drawer, find there are no clean ones left and then look through laundry basket for the least dirty one there.
15. Hold the baby in one hand and the 16 used nappy sacks in the other and carry them back to the living room.
16. React calmly when your wife sniffs and says the child has already pooped again and needs changing.
17. Repeat for next two years.

Why won't the ungrateful thing look at me?

Babies are often born with two eyes, but for the first few weeks, they point blank refuse to use them properly. In fact, despite the fact you are giving this thing so much love and attention, it won't even look at you, let alone smile. All that coochie cooing and singing Leonard Cohn songs and all it does is look everywhere except actually at you.

Your first thought will be that it must be autistic, or possibly blind. It's probably best not to articulate this initially even if this means you can't then say 'I told you so' if it's proved to be true.

The next thought will be that you're doing something wrong, and that therefore the baby is not bonding with you. This is unlikely as well as month-old kids aren't particularly discerning when choosing their entertainment*

Hopefully your final thought will be that it is still too young to be able to focus properly and that if it could talk, it would tell you how appreciative it is of your baby talk.

Once you have established eye contact, there is another issue – it can't smile. Or so it wants you to believe.

* But still don't show them anything starring Adam Sandler

No matter how hilarious your peek-a-boo is, the baby will stare blankly at you with a look that could be interpreted as a bit pitying. *

Again, keep calm and don't assume that it is brain damaged or slow. However if it still hasn't smile by the time it reaches puberty assume there may be an issue**

Babies usually smile at about four to six weeks. The first time it happens is a magical moment you'll never forget, but is probably caused by trapped wind.

After that, the crying to laughing ratio is about forty-to-one, so savour them as much as you can.

Feeding & weaning it

OK, so let's remember that it's no longer an 'it'. It's a he or she. And he or she will need food.

This is a key moment for the father because a new mum has to decide whether or not to breast feed. And if she does, that immediately excuses you from all night feeds for six months or more.

Think about that for a few moments – instead of being jabbed in the ribs every few hours to get up, find a sterilized bottle and sit in the dark trying to get a few milliliters down its throat, you will be snuggled under a warm duvet.

If only you had lactating breasts you'd be there like a shot, but evolution cruelly robbed you of the opportunity. So instead it's your wife who has to do every single night feed.

But, what if she decides against breastfeeding? This is a horror too, er, horrific to think about for too long, so you need to have a response ready.

* Get used to this as your teenage kids will do exactly the same as we'll see later
** Or it's an emo

Reasons why she should breast feed

1. It's free. And now the baby is happily raiding the contents of your savings account in so many other ways, here's a God given opportunity to claw some back
2. No endless sterilising of bottles and teats.
3. If you run out of normal milk on a Sunday morning, you can pop a couple of drops in your coffee.
4. Her pregnant belly is gone and the swollen up boobs stay swollen giving her the cleavage she (you) always dreamed of .
5. There are starving babies in Africa*
6. It will help her bond with her baby
7. Her friends will respect her more
8. It's what Lorraine Kelly would have done
9. Breastfed babies are 13% more intelligent, 36% more likely to compete in the Olympics and cry 105% less than bottlefed babies**. So denying them a sup at the nipple is tantamount to child abuse.
10. The Bible specifically instructs all mothers to 'let thine babies take unto thou plentiful breast for it is the word of our lord who art so bountiful'***.

If that doesn't do the trick, then you might be stuck with several sleepless nights. And after all that work you did in picking the wife up from hospital, getting in a load of shopping from Asda and doing your own washing for three days, hardly seems fair.

* This is a useful phrase to drop in, even though technically it doesn't mean very much. Arguably the babies in Africa would be starving whether or not she breastfeeds.
** All percentages are approximate, and have only a casual relationship with the truth
*** Deuteronomy 23: 13-14 (but don't bother looking it up)

Using bottles does mean that every single piece of equipment, including the dummies, needs sterilising within an inch of its life. These days you either bung the sterilizer in the microwave or plug it in. Then, using the pair of tongs (which has also been heat treated) you pull each teat onto the screw top and put in an exact amount of the formula milk into the bottle with recently boiled water.

By child number two, you're a little bit more relaxed and if a teat accidentally touches the work surface or the number of granules of powder isn't exact, you can live with it. When baby number three shows up, you're wrestling the dummy off the dog and sticking it into the child's mouth to shut it up.

Whether or not she breastfeeds, the good thing about the first four months or so is that the smell of poo isn't too bad. After all, its only ingredient is milk, so is smells like a mild cheese or vanilla ice cream. However, don't be tempted to taste it.

After you introduce solids at around six months, it's a whole new ball game. It smells like shit.

The nursery

Your house may have had three bedrooms, but now it has two and a nursery. Even though the baby can hardly focus beyond the end of its nose and would be just at home in a temperature controlled janitor's cupboard, you will be expected to completely redecorate every aspect of this room.

And there's no point in suggesting that the baby is too busy sleeping and vomiting to notice the Spongebob Squarepants frieze and matching lightshade.

Every object in the room must be transformed. The chest of drawers will need primary colours all over it, the carpet must contain at least one Pixar character and the door cannot remain plain old white – it needs stickers of farm animals applied liberally.

Even the ceiling doesn't escape. Special glow in the dark stars must be affixed to keep the baby entertained when it's not gazing at its flashing Shrek mobile spinning over the cot.

If the overall effect looks like a Mad Hatter's acid trip, then you've succeeded.

The added complication is that you can't actually start the decorating until you know the sex of the baby. And if you've chosen not to find out, you'll have a race on your hands as soon as it's delivered.

Any trace of pink in a boy's room will inevitably make him a member of the transgender community while a blue item for a girl will make her aggressive towards her dolls.

A slight get out clause here is to decorate the room in yellows, greens or earthy colours, but then one of the grandmothers will comment that it's such a pity that you couldn't have found out what you were having as the room 'just doesn't look right'.

Naturally enough, once the baby is old enough to speak, he will demand that the whole room be redecorated as 'Teletubbies are so 2008' and, anyway, he's already ripped most of the wallpaper off and scribbled all over the door and carpet in red permanent marker pen.

Perhaps the miracle of fatherhood can best be expressed with a couple of simple charts to show the subtle changes in your life now compared to a year ago when you were a carefree couple.

A man's life before kids
    19% in bed
    13% deciding what to do when you get out of bed
    7% playing sport
    10% romantic nights out
    9% Wild, passionate sex
    12% Boozy nights out with mates
    5% recovering from boozy nights out with mates
    10% Relaxing foreign holidays

15% cinema, theatre, art galleries, shopping, leisurely walks in country

A man's life during the 1st year of fatherhood
5% in bed
2% in bed actually asleep
26% apologizing for incidents that probably weren't your fault
21% sterilizing bottles & dummies, and then resterilising them when they are immediately dropped on the floor
6% changing nappies
13% clearing up vomit, poo, piss, broken crockery and dropped food
14% Rocking baby to sleep (and failing)
2% planning urgent vasectomy
10% praying for the screaming to end
0.6% nights out boring mates with 'hilarious' anecdotes about your baby.
0.3% romantic nights out with half-asleep wife
0.1% Token attempt at sex

6

Toddlers

"If evolution really works, how come mothers only have two hands?"
*~ **Milton Berle***

"My father only hit me once - but he used a Volvo"
*~ **Bob Monkhouse***

Like sea creatures emerging from the Paleolithic swamps, so harmless babies grow muscles and bone density so they can sit up, crawl and finally walk. This is very inconvenient.

A bag of spew sitting safely on a playmat is one thing, when it can manoeuvre itself up stairs, under cars and towards swimming pools, it's another.

Your baby has become fascinated by its surroundings and wants to explore. And by 'explore', I of course mean destroy.

Unfortunately modern child rearing manuals frown upon keeping them in a cage for prolonged periods, so you're going to have to adapt your lovely house.

There are some items you'll need to get rid of immediately:

1. All those expensive bone china ornaments you've collected.
2. The cream-coloured rug
3. The cream-coloured dog

4. The goldfish bowl
5. The koi pond
6. Garden gnomes
7. Ornamental samurai sword

Pretty much every house has at least one of all of the above. And, no, barbecued koi carp don't taste nearly as nice as you'd think, so do the right thing and release them into the sea.

Then there are the other hazards:

1. **The stairs.**

    If you cared about the welfare of your toddler, you'd move to a bungalow, but failing that, the only other thing is to seal off the steps using stair gates fitted with either barbed wire or a small electricity charge. This will also dissuade any passing farm animals from attempting to go upstairs.

2. **The garden**

    You'd think it'd be perfectly safe to leave a small child outside for a few minutes to play with the nettles and adders, but oh no. So-called 'childcare experts' would have us believe that we need to monitor them at all times. And tethering them is considered inappropriate as well, even if you've left them a bowl of water and a piece of asbestos roofing to shade under.

3. **The TV**

    The TV is your friend, and will probably play a greater role in bringing up your child than you do, but it is also fraught with danger. Firstly there are so many fun games to be played with all those wires hanging out the back. But putting your child *in front* of the telly could be even worse if they end up watching Jeremy Kyle or Made in Chelsea.

4. **The main road**
    We give kids toy cars, so who can blame them for being fascinated with real ones. And the only place to find any decent ones is on a nice stretch of tarmac just a few metres from the front door. And who can resist that whoosh whooshing sound as they go past? The only realistic solution here is to join the Amish and renounce the internal combustion engine.

5. **The pit bull terrier**
    These cute-as-a-button cuddly family pooches are also in grave danger from the toddler. Just make sure you've got your camcorder ready when the little tyke tries to poke the dog's eye out or steal a bone from it. Priceless memories.

First words

By the time the kid is two, it should be making a lot of noise. In its mind, it is making perfect sense so it's very frustrating when you fail to grasp that it has asked you for a bottle or another donut or to pass the remote.

Then, the sounds get a little more word-like. They're still largely unintelligible, but, like anything said by Keith Richards, you know there is an attempt at meaning in there somewhere.

Luckily, nature has decreed that there's a good chance that the word 'daddy' will be said weeks ahead of 'mummy'. This is almost certainly because the child, even now, recognizes that you are its most important and most loved parent. So feel quietly smug, and don't mention it to the missus.

Other parents will also want to know what the first word was. This is another good chance for one upmanship. Don't tell them it was 'duck', 'daddy', 'no', 'again' or 'Bieber' as these are far too boring. Instead make out the first utterance was something more meaningful demonstrating that your offspring is destined for greatness.

Words like: 'Benjamin Britten', 'Flanders', 'Churchill', 'Botham', 'Kelly Brook', 'Gazza' or 'Paralympics' will lead to knowing nods that you have a very special child, albeit a show off.

Can we get someone else to look after it please?

Unless you and your wife are shipwrecked on a remote desert island with your child, there is every chance that at some point another responsible adult will look after it.

And, yes, I did call you responsible.

Babysitters

Prior to having kids, most people assume that before leaving their child with a babysitter, they would want full police checks, seven written references, passport verification and proof that they are trained in CPR.

After the sprog appears, however, the desire to escape for a few hours means you'll resort to roaming the streets asking hobos if they can spare a few minutes to sit for you. And the 17-year-old crystal meth dealer next door from the skinhead gang suddenly seems a decent option.

To your wife, he might seem a safer bet than his leggy blonde sister in the crop top and short shorts.

In all seriousness, you do need to carefully vet all potential babysitters by getting them to fill in this questionnaire:

1. If the child is sick I will:
a) Call the parents
b) Call my dealer to get rid of the evidence

2. If it's an emergency, I will:
a) Dial 999, apply pressure to the wound and give mouth to mouth if necessary.
b) Gently tell the child that my Jehovah's Witness faith prevents me from letting him go to hospital to have a transfusion.

3. If he needs a bedtime story, I'll read:
a) Paddington Bear
b) 50 Shades of Grey

4. The only thing I will watch on TV is:
a) Nickelodeon
b) The sex tape I found under your bed

5. Lights out will be:
a) As soon as the little one closes his tired eyes
b) When the police helicopter is circling overhead

6. My hourly rate is:
a) £15
b) Negotiated by my pimp

7. If you're back after midnight:
a) I might have fallen asleep on the sofa
b) I might have to invite my first client round here

8. If the poor little girl gets scared, I will:
a) Stroke her hand until she drifts off to sleep
b) Put away the whip and handcuffs

9. Her boyfriend is:
a) A local boy studying medicine
b) Alex Reid

Mostly As

Don't trust her – she's lying. If something sounds too good to be true, it probably is. Except Olivia Newton-John, that is. Call the police if you think she's offering her services around the neighbourhood.

Mostly Bs
Her refreshing honesty means that you can trust her completely. A girl who is obviously a hard worker, flexible, devout and good with money is someone your toddler can learn look up to and idolise. In fact ask her if she'd consider being a live-in nanny before she's snapped up by someone else.

What if the babysitter is hot?
This can be a very dangerous circumstance for the father. One that needs to be handled with care lest it create an awkward situation. If the young girl you've invited into your home to look after your kids is hot, you need to take stock of the potential fallout from making the wrong call. You best plan therefore is to open a window. If she's still hot, she can remove her coat.

Childminders
These are people who have actually chosen to spend more time with children than is absolutely necessary. So a degree of suspicion is in order. If you and your wife are both working all hours to fed your new found family, then you may have to farm the kid out to one during daylight hours*

When you go to meet them, they will explain about all the interactive equipment they provide for the children – painting, clay modeling, dressing up, story time, building bricks and cooking - and show you the nutritious meals that are cooked freshly to order every day using organic fruit and veg and free range meats.

As soon as they have your child in their clutches however, they are plonked in front of Cartoon Network with a bag of chips and some Sainsbury's Basics custard creams. Ten minutes before pick up time, the telly goes off and a few craft materials are scattered around the room. Your children are warned to keep quiet or they'll be sent to a childminder who'll make them eat broccoli.

* Most stubbornly refuse to have them during the night too. Selfish.

Nursery

These are a bit more fun for the kid. For a start there are lots more of their kind to play with and steal their (more tasty) lunch. Nurseries are manned by acne-plagued staff, who appear to be only a couple of years older than the tallest children there.

Their hours are deliberately designed to be annoying, as opening at 8am means you'll probably be late for work and you'll also need to leave early to get back for 6pm. It would be much more convenient of they picked up the kids (still in their pyjamas) nice and early, and then delivered them back asleep (back in pjs) in the evening. That way there is no need for you to have to rearrange that early meeting or miss out on Jonno's leaving drinks.

But, alas, this isn't going to happen while the 'do gooders' have their way and write books about children needing two loving parents to look after them and nurture them through their early years. Oh yeah – well who was looking after *their* kids while they were writing the books, eh? Hypocrites.

Taking toddlers on holiday

A common mistake parents of toddlers make is going on holiday expecting it to be relaxing. Two weeks in the sun, they reason, is just what the family needs to recharge their batteries and get away from the chaos of every day life. They hark back to the days spent lazing by the pool with a pina colada, Stephen King novel and sunglasses dark enough so the teenage girls walking past can't see you staring. They remember the nights out in the local bars, supping too much local beer, dancing, romantically strolling along the beach and then collapsing until midday with a stinging hangover and mild alcohol poisoning.

Those days have gone for about twenty years. The next time you have a holiday like that you will be in your late sixties and when you laze by the pool, it'll be with three types of medication, a large print novel, a urinary tract infection and sunglasses dark enough so the middle aged women walking past can't see you staring.

To illustrate this point, take this diary of a holiday taken by a typical family – husband, wife and kids aged three and seven months.

Tuesday June 1st
Only three days to go now until our week in Lanzarote! Vicky and I are so excited, and I think Jack and Hatty are too in their own way.

Wednesday June 2nd
We did the holiday shopping today. To be honest, we spent far more than I thought we would – swim nappies, sunsuits, portable bottle sterilizer, sun hats, inflatable life preservers, kiddies sun block, lightweight pushchair, UV resistant sun pod, new carrycot, first aid kit, baby and toddler sunglasses and rubber shoes for the beach. Not to mention all the baby food, new clothes and nappies. I asked Vicky if I could buy a new pair of shorts but she said they would cost too much.

Thursday June 3rd
One day to go! Had to buy a new suitcase today to fit everything in. Vicky wants to take a few of Jack's cuddly toys and books so he doesn't get homesick and said that I should be able to fit my clothes into my hand luggage. Had a sleepless night because Hatty was running a temperature and just wouldn't drop off.

Friday June 4th
Well, I'm writing this in our hotel room. Can't believe we're finally here after all those long weeks of waiting.

Had a bit of a drama getting to the airport as the taxi didn't have the baby seat we'd requested. The second one had one though – it just didn't have the toddler one. By the time a third had been dispatched, we were running very late. We'd dressed Hatty in a lovely pink cardigan her gran had knitted, but she was sick pretty much as soon as we got to the terminal and Vicky said she'd never get the sick out, so we had to dump it. Sorry Mum!

Jack then dissolved in tears because Daddy had forgotten his chew rag. Vicky said that I could go back to get it and then catch a later flight1 I laughed, but turned out she was being serious. Luckily, we distracted him with a bag of lollies.

The man sat next to me on the plane was quite rude after Hatty was sick all over him. It wasn't as though I hadn't warned him. I had turned to stop Jack throwing another cup of juice at the flight attendant and unfortunately had positioned Hatty so she was pointing right at him. I'd run out of bibs by then, so had a few sheets of toilet paper stuffed into the top of the babygro which had by now turned into a putrid mulsh.

Jack demanded more sweets, but I told him he'd had quite enough and he could have a banana instead. At this point, Hatty started her screaming. You could hardy blame her as she wasn't feeling well, but the passengers around me kept glaring at me as if it were my fault.

Then one of them pointed out that there was a very strong smell of poo coming from her nappy, which I hadn't noticed because there was so much sick over my t-shirt as well as Jack's orange juice all over my lap.

I gave Jack the rest of the lollies and stood to take Hatty to the toilet with a new nappy and some new clothes as turned out they were filthy too. The man next to me hadn't noticed a slight brown smear on the arm of his suit luckily.

I told Jack not to wake up his mum or else I'd take the treats away.

In the toilet, I cleaned her bottom and managed to put on the new nappy (backwards, but I was sure it would still work). I needed a wee so I kept one hand on Hatty on her change shelf and used the other to aim. Unfortunately she got bored and tried to roll off. I caught her, but also peed all over my trousers quite badly, which was embarrassing.

For the next three hours, I bounced Hatty up and down on one knee while Jack balanced on the other. I tried singing to them, reading them a story, giving them the sick bags to play with, but nothing worked. Even when the meal arrived, Jack refused to eat anything so

I had to give in and hand him a packet of Starburst. For some reason that made him even more hyperactive. You really can't win!

By the time the pilot told us we were starting our descent, the man in the suit had discovered the poo on his sleeve and made quite a fuss. He even suggested that I pay for it to be dry cleaned, but I pretended not to hear as Hatty was red in the face howling and Jack was jumping up and down on his seat singing Gangnam Style as loudly as he could.

Just as the wheels touched down, they both fell sound asleep and Vicky yawned loudly and woke up. She looked at the kids and said we were lucky they were such good flyers.

At the baggage reclaim we discovered the airline had lost the pushchair, so I had to carry Jack and the cases while Vicky pushed Hatty to the coach in the pram.

The hotel is amazing – right on the beach with two pools, great restaurants, lots of palm trees and even a golf course next door, which is very handy!

Our room is smaller than I expected. The lady at reception told us they didn't get many young children so they had put us in a twin room with a mattress on the floor and a space to wedge the cot against the bathroom door.

I'm the only one left awake now – and I'm completely shattered. All I have to do before turning in is sterilize the bottles for morning, put the cot together (Hatty's in my bed for now), find a washing machine to clean all the clothes soaked in vomit, urine, orange juice and blood (I gashed my shin on a step carrying the kids up the nine flights to our room as Vicky said the lift was a bit noisy and might wake them).

Saturday June 5th

The sun is shining, the pool looks gorgeous and there's a beer with my name on it at the swim up bar!

Both kids were up most of the night. As one got to sleep the other would stir and wake the up again. It was like a relay, but luckily Vicky slept through it. By 5am they were both wide awake and demanding breakfast, but that doesn't start until 7am so I spent two hours walking round trying to get them to have a snooze.

It was then I found out that the kids club is closed this week. Apparently our tour company should have told us, but they must have forgotten.

After breakfast, we all went down to the pool. It took about an hour to get all the stuff we needed together. As soon as we arrived, I had to go back to the room as Hatty needed changing and I'd forgotten the wipes. I was gently lowering Jack into the water when a waiter said that children weren't allowed in this pool and we'd have to go to the Kiddies Fun Pool, which sounded like it might be exciting. Vicky suggested I take them over while she has a rest and we could swap later.

Getting to the pool was very easy – it was down the drive, out of the main gate, past the goods delivery depot and then round the back of the staff quarters. Definitely less than a kilometer. I hoped there might be a swim up bar there, but there wasn't really enough water to actually swim as such. There was a helpful workman using a pneumatic drill to break up some concrete who said that the pool was very nearly finished and we were welcome to use it. He said that if the kids' eyes turned red, it was because he might have put too much chlorine in by mistake.

If I wanted towels, or a lounger, I'd have to go back to the other pool.

Well, the kids had a lovely time splashing about. Jack laughed so much when I stood on a piece of masonry at the bottom of the pool and disappeared underwater. I had to get out for a time to let the bleeding stop.

We only had to nip back to the other pool three times – once to get another bottle of milk, once because Jack wanted to do a 'Number two' (which he did half way back) and again when Jack realised he'd forgotten his rubber ball.

By then Vicky had gone to have lunch at the Mongolian barbeque. I fancied the same, but it had closed by then so I had a jar of Hatty's pureed pumpkin instead, which certainly filled a gap!

Vicky suggested it might be an idea for me to push the kids round a bit to get them to have their afternoon nap. Well, about an hour later they were finally both dozing peacefully - right until a large Spanish woman yelled 'Hola!' at them and insisted on a cuddle.

Luckily it only took another hour to get them in the land of nod. I crept back to the pool and Vicky said she didn't mind looking after them for a while. I was going to have a well-earned beer, but Vicky pointed out that now I'd eaten the pumpkin, we'd need more baby food so I'd have to pop to the shops. She also reminded me that I would need to sterilize two more bottles.

So I hopped on a bus to the main town and less than two hours later I was back, just as the kids were waking and Vicky said I could take over as she had booked a facial at the spa.

Anyway, it was a very full day and we were all glad of our bed! As Jack is a restless sleeper, Vicky decided that he'd be better off in my bed and I could have the mattress on the floor.

Sunday June 6th

Kids up at 4.30am this morning, so an even longer trek round the grounds. We'd booked an excursion today to see the volcano, an amazing trip my parents told me about and I'd been dying to see for years. Unfortunately when we got on the coach, the driver said the trip wasn't suitable for children under six, and that the booking desk should have told us, but must have forgotten. They also said there was no question of a refund. Vicky said she didn't mind going on her own as then I'd get more bonding time with the kids.

I tried taking them to the beach, but Jack saw a crab and refused to set foot on the sand again. Hatty needed changing anyway, so we headed back to the room and ended up watching TV for most of the day until Vicky got home and told me that I was being mean keeping them out of the sunshine so we headed out again while she took a nap. Jack pointed at the restaurant very excitedly, so I took them there. As Hatty was in a highchair and therefore taking up a place I was told I would have to order a meal for her. So she had fish and chips and ate about half a chip before being sick down her bib. Jack said he wanted a burger, but changed his mind when it arrived and was playing up so badly I didn't even get a chance to take a bite from my steak.

Monday June 7th

Hatty is running another temperature. Vicky says it's my fault for forcing her to eat chips so I'll have to stay with her while she sleeps. As Jack was being naughty, Vicky told him that as a punishment for making her late to her pedicure, he'd have to stay in the room with us too.

Tuesday June 8th

We decided to go on an excursion to a secluded bay for a spot of snorkeling. Vicky asked me to pop back into town to buy both kids expensive wetsuits and snorkeling gear. I did protest that Hatty was a little young, but Vicky said I should have more faith in my children.

Anyway, I got back just after lunch and ran to the pier where the boat was waiting. The bay was about a half hour away, so we used that time to get the kids ready, even though I was very seasick and must have been sick over the side about fifteen times.

When we got there, Hatty was asleep and Jack said the water was too wet for him and started screaming that he wanted to go back to the hotel.

Vicky said she didn't mind if I went back with them both, so, while everyone went off to look for fish, we were put on another dinghy and taken back to shore.

It wasn't a total disaster, though, as Vicky said she saw thousands of tropical fish and had been given a sumptuous lunch with wine and beer thrown in. She even brought me back some lobster to try, although I've tasted better to be honest.

Wednesday June 9th
Woke up at 2am with crippling stomach pains. Threw my guts up in the toilet and genuinely thought I was going to die. The pain was unbelievable and I was vomiting blood at one point. I yelled out for Vicky to call reception to get an ambulance. I have to say she was great – she jumped into action and said that I'd be more comfortable one of the sofas in reception where there was less chance of me waking the kids. She volunteered to stay in the room while I made my way downstairs. She told me I should clean up the bathroom first as the smell was pretty terrible. I did my best, but was bent over double, still puking green bile every couple of minutes – all of which had to be cleaned up.

I crawled to the lift, then collapsed again. When I came to, I was in the back of an ambulance being given oxygen. The side of my head hurt and I figured I must have landed heavily when I fell.

A nurse told me I was in a coma for the rest of the day. I begged her to ring Vicky as I knew how worried she'd be. The message can't have got through though, because there was no sign of her.

Thursday June 10th
Still felt like death. The doctor diagnosed food poisoning and said I was lucky to be alive. He ordered bed rest for at least a week, but I knew I couldn't leave Vicky on her own to look after the kids.

I checked myself out and got a cab back to the hotel. I found Vicky by the pool having a foot massage. I could tell she was concerned because she insisted I go straight back to the room and rest. She pointed out that I could relieve the babysitter as she was costing us €16 an hour.

As soon as I got there, Jack decided he was hungry and Hatty needed a feed. Vicky hadn't had time to get the bottles prepared so I washed and sterilised them as best I could, all the time still feeling like my stomach lining was on fire. Jack was bouncing off the walls so I had to take him downstairs to see if I could get him a snack. The café was closed and all the gift shop had was lollies. I bought him another tube of Starburst while trying to stop Hatty screaming for her milk. I could smell that she'd pooped, but hadn't realised until that moment that she wasn't wearing a nappy. The fact it was dripping out onto my hand also told me that she was still feeling ill.

I somehow tore two leg holes in the gift shop bag and put her inside it until we could get back to the room. I was too weak to carry her so I used a hotel luggage trolley to push her.

At the room, I soon saw that we were out of nappies. The smell was so bad that I think I passed out a couple of times as I tried to undress and wash her.

I tied a hand towel around her bottom and staggered back to the lobby to ask if there was anywhere in the hotel that sold nappies. There wasn't, so I had to walk to the bus stop with both children screaming and go into the town. The driver had to stop twice for me to be sick, which was good of him.

An hour later we were back. A kindly couple carried the kids for me as I couldn't actually walk. After dragging myself along the roadside for about two hundred metres, I pulled myself upright to cross the road to the reception, but blacked out again. Luckily the concierge had found a babysitter to take the kids back to the room.

The hotel doctor was called and said I had to go to hospital immediately, but Hatty needed another bottle by then and Jack still hadn't had his lunch, so I told him I was feeling OK.

My shirt was torn and covered in mud and vomit and had blood stains where I'd cut my arm on some broken glass. I took it off and crawled back to the room.

As I opened the door, I could see Vicky had made it back from the pool.

'I thought I said we can't afford endless babysitters,' she snapped. 'And I see you've been sunbathing. It's all right for some, isn't it? Well, it's time for you to take your turn and look after the children for once. I'm going to a basket weaving demonstration by the pool.'

Friday June 11th

I felt a bit better today, just in time for the journey home. Can't believe we've been here a week already. I packed the bags and was about to ring for a porter to take them down when Vicky said that I shouldn't treat the hotel staff like slaves. So I carried Hatty in one hand, Jack on my shoulders, a case in the other hand and managed to push the other one in front of me to the lift. Vicky said she'd reserve us a couple of sunbeds by the pool so we could soak up a few last rays.

As it turned out, once I'd gone back up for the hand luggage, sterilized more bottles, fed Hatty, bought Jack another packet of Starburst, changed Hatty twice, soaked her dirty clothes, spun them in the tumble dryer, fed Hatty, changed Jack, found three socks in lost property, checked out, sterilized two more bottles using a plug in the lobby, paid for Vicky's beauty treatments and changed my shirt, which Hatty had been sick over, it was time to leave.

Luckily Vicky got another good sleep on the plane and only three passengers complained this time (four if you count the steward who tripped over Jack's leg).

Saturday June 12th

The holiday is over already! It was certainly great to get away for a few days of relaxation, and to spend some quality time with the children. Vicky told me she's already booked for us to go again next year.

Holidays with toddlers are about as relaxing as spending time in a warzone – except the noise and suffering are far worse. So does that mean holidays are out of the question for the foreseeable future?

Well, yes. Although there is one very useful trick you can use to make things a little easier – invite your parents.

After all, they too want to spend quality time with their grandchildren. And, hopefully 'quantity time' too so that you and your wife can still go for those romantic walks, enjoy a few drinks, laze by the pool etc.

Better still – they take the kids away while the two of you relax at home. It'll be more of a holiday than an actual holiday.

But, hang on a second, we're painting a very negative picture here. Toddlers aren't *all* bad, well, most aren't anyway. In fact they can be very cute and entertaining. That said, the key point to take away is that going away to Paradise itself isn't going to be much fun if there's no kids club or children's menu.

Should we have another kid?

This is a question that will push its way to the front of your mind as your adorable firstborn reaches his or her second birthday. After all, your wife's not getting any younger, and you don't want a screwed up only child, do you?

Or do you?

Consider this…

Advantages of only children
1. No squabbling between siblings
2. Less chance of your kid being a serial killer/terrorist/member of The Wiggles
3. Less cash spent on food
4. No need to move to bigger house
5. You can blame their personality disorders on them being an only child instead of your bad parenting
6. Less money spent on Christmas/birthday presents
7. Their imaginary friend will cut down on phone bills to actual friends

8. Eliminates possibility of two of your kids marrying each other and having a brood of freaks
9. Reduction in money spent via Tooth Fairy.

Disadvantages of only children
1. Fewer offspring to look after you in your dotage
2. If this one malfunctions, no back up
3. More money spent on psychologists
4. He has no one to play with, so need to bus-in friends
5. Kick arounds in the back yard less fun with only two (particularly if it's a girl).
6. All your friends will pity you, assume you have a low sperm count and/or impotence, and therefore couldn't father any more.
7. No one to carry on your family name if it's a girl. *

If you decide to have another baby solely on the basis that there are more advantages printed here than disadvantages (and that's as good a reason as any), then the next thing is the timing. Should you pressure your wife to get pregnant as soon as her stitches have healed, or wait until the firstborn starts school to make things easier?

Kids who are close in age
GOOD: Socks, undies, t-shirts interchangeable so saves money
BAD: Two screaming kids under two is more than twice as bad as one screaming kid under two

GOOD: They become good mates and entertain each other
BAD: They become mortal enemies and you're the UN peacekeeper

* This could be considered an advantage if your surname is Cockrot or Stiffy

GOOD: You get the full-on, stressful years out of the way quicker
BAD: The full-on, stressful years are twice as full-on and stressful

GOOD: They both become old enough to watch violent movies with you earlier thereby cutting out the need to see *Cinderella III: The Fairy Prince* at the Odeon.
BAD: They steal your stash of porn DVDs that much earlier

Kids who are *not* close in age
GOOD: You save money as one gets to babysit the other
BAD: The school run could last twenty years

GOOD: The teachers might have forgotten how hideous your first child was by the time the second is in their class
BAD: If the three of you are seen out together, you might be mistaken for the granddad.

GOOD: The first can have the birds and bees talk with his younger sibling, thereby relieving you of the embarrassment
BAD: He might be a little too graphic and leave you to answer the awkward questions like 'Why would condoms need to be flavoured?'

GOOD: If you have about ten kids, you can form a singing group, shag the nanny and successfully flee the Nazis
BAD: If the gap is too big, you could be forced to bounce a baby on your replacement knee

OK, but how many should we have?
We've covered off whether you're going to add to your burden, er, I mean family, but then the same question will rear up in a couple of years. With outstanding genes like yours is it really fair on the world if you only have two?

There are millions of third children who have gone on to greatness. Just think - if all parents had stopped at two we wouldn't have had Jim Carrey, Margaret Thatcher, Adolf Hitler or Danny Devito.

Er, actually don't think about that. I'm sure there are plenty of other better examples, um, somewhere.

Anyway, hopefully this guide will help you see things a little clearer:

1 child

There is plenty of evidence that not all only children become psychotic nut jobs, cut off from polite society, resentful of their parents and quietly planning their first high school shooting. Some also become bankers, traffic wardens, and journalists.

2 children

Only having one sibling means they will vie for your attention, be violently competitive and plot each other's downfall. If one is more gifted, the other will sink into a pit of self-doubt and loathing and get regression therapy in later life to see if they can pin anything on you.

3 children

You create the 'middle child'. He or she isn't the go-getting first born who takes on the world and becomes a captain of industry, nor is he the cute baby of the family who gets all the cuddles. No, he is in his own, lonely world. On the upside he has low expectations on Christmas and birthdays so you get to save some money.

4 children

So now you have *two* middle children. How could you?

5 children

If you have five of the same sex, you have a ready made netball or basketball team, or, better still, get them to form a harmonious singing group with the cute little one put under enormous pressure as lead singer. Just don't be shocked when he befriends a monkey and writes you out of his will.

6 children

We're getting towards old woman in shoe territory here. Six kids means that you may well be an excellent Catholic, but you're also going to be poor.

More than 6 kids

Unless you accidentally had octuplets, this smacks of bad planning. If you really do have your heart set on this many, you may want to convert to Mormonism and have more than one wife.

School

"My school was so tough the school newspaper had an obituary section."
~ Norm Crosby

"I distrust anybody who thought school was a good time."
~ Stephen King

The first day

Chances are you can remember that fateful morning when your loving mum strapped you into the car and then dumped you sobbing at the gates of a Dickensian jail that she referred to as 'school'.

Unlike your cosy pre-school where you got an afternoon nap and spent all day having fun, this place had rows of wooden desks in draughty classrooms presided over by a woman who glared at you over her glasses if you put your hand up to ask to go to the toilet and made you do something she called 'work'.

The other children stole your lunch, pulled your hair, said you were fat, dacked you and called you a 'Poo poo head'.

At 3pm, your mother picked you up and informed you that you'd be going back to this place every single day for the next twelve years and that these will be the best years of their lives.

This can be a little disconcerting for a five-year-old.

But, you, as the dad, can be there to reassure that it might not be as bad as it seems, and that there are some upsides of school. Like, er, the summer holidays.

Your first child starting school can be an emotional time. It seems like only five years earlier that you were cradling a newborn, and now it has taken its first tentative steps towards independence.

Your role will be to take a photo in their crisp, new uniform and then ring home to ask how it went and sound excited and impressed at whatever you're told, even though the entire school day will have been forgotten and they'll already be watching a DVD while they're talking to you.

Is your child a genius... or thick as shit?

Most people agree the major problem with the state school system is that pupils get taught far too much. Fair enough, teach them to read, add up and the name of the capital of Burkina Faso, but all that other stuff?

It's no wonder that some kids struggle and are labeled failures before they can even spell it.

And it's not always easy to tell if your happy little chappy inherited your high degree of intelligence (and probably good looks) or whether they copped a load of defective genes from Great Uncle Clyde on their mother's side.

It can therefore come as a terrible shock the first time you meet the teacher when she *doesn't* tell you that your child is top of the class.

Look out for a few of these phrases used by kindly teachers to gently break the news that you perhaps don't need to start a uni fund:

Ah, we all love Kevin. He's just so... special

Chloe is coming on well. Just yesterday she remembered her name
Oh, you're Connor's father. I'm so sorry
Be assured we will do our best for Sam and see what we can salvage
She's so sporty. What a shame the Paralympics is only for *physical* disabilities
Well, your son is wrong to feel stupid. We prefer moronic.
Just last week he was on top of the class! But we did ask him to climb back down.
Don't knock being bottom of the class – the only way is up! Or sideways.
It may be best for him to repeat his pre-school class a few times. At least until his beard makes it too obvious

This can be devastating. But, on the upside, stupid people are happier in life as they have no expectations. And who needs all that career stress when they could be working in the good ol' outdoors. Those ditches aren't going to dig themselves!

However, to avoid the shock of being told this, there are ways you can test your child prior to the first day at school. Start with this test. You'll need to read it to them as they can't recognize actual words yet. If they can write already, don't bother with the test.

1. What is 1 + 1?
a) 2
b) 3
c) This is boring. I want some crips.

2. What is long, yellow, a bit bent and yummy to munch on
a) A banana
b) An orange
c) That thing in Mummy's bedside drawer

3. What's the difference between a dog and a cat?
a) One goes woof and the other miaow
b) They are the same
c) You never call Mummy an 'old cat'.

4. What is the best thing on TV?
a) Scooby Doo
b) That photo frame
c) The video of you and Mummy wrestling naked

5. What's the longest word you know?
a) Antidisestablishmentarianism
b) Longest
c) McDonald's

6. Finish this sentence: I love The Cat In The…
a) Hat
b) Charlotte's Web
c) Microwave

Mostly As

Apart from a worrying need to comply, probably stemming from deep-seated insecurities and inner turmoil, your child is also what is known in the scientific community as a 'swot'. Don't expect a big turn out for his birthday party.

Mostly Bs

Teachers love a blank canvass, uncorrupted by knowledge, onto which they can impart their knowledge. And your child is certainly blank.

Mostly Cs

Street smart, switched on and mature beyond their years – your child is none of these. Buy him a dog so somebody loves him.

Can you make your child smarter?

This is a question many dads ask. More accurately they ask: is there a way I can make him/her smarter with minimal effort and no loss of cash?

Well, the answer is yes. You don't have to sit back and accept a dunce; you can be the great father you always knew you would be by following these steps:

1. Reading a book takes ages. Better to get the kid to watch the film adaptation so it only takes a couple of hours.
2. Doing homework never helped anyone. Luckily there are now some great websites that will do it for them. Best to get them to skim read it before handing it in though
3. If they are worried about a big exam, simply get them to take a sickie so they can't flunk it
4. Doing sport is all very well, but the same skills can be learned by playing the Xbox or Wii equivalent sport game from the comfort and safety of an armchair. Better still – get them some chips to eat while they're playing
5. Nothing broadens the mind more than travelling the world. As plane tickets cost money, there is a ready made alternative: Google Earth. They can literally see anywhere on the planet and imagine what it must be like to go there.
6. Fruit and veg are hardly very tasty, are they? Offer a child a choice between broccoli and Kinder Surprise and I think we know which they'll choose – and who are we to persuade them otherwise? So you'll feel a lot less guilty about feeding them junk food if you give them a few vitamins to take as well. Remember – it's not called a 'Happy Meal' for nothing.
7. In an ideal world we'd have the time to read a book to them at night, but we have work to do, important clients to call, games to watch etc. A perfect alternative is an audiobook. Start with

Gordon Brown reading his memoir and if that doesn't work, move on to Jack Straw's. If they're not asleep after that, call an ambulance.

Bullying: a bad thing?

No one likes a bully. Though, to be fair, a lot of people *pretend* to like them so as not to be beaten to a pulp. And pretend friends are better than no friends at all, right?

Wrong! Well, partially wrong anyway.

For a father, there is only one thing worse than finding out that you child is being bullied: finding out your child is the bully.

If he's being bullied, then you can remonstrate with the other parents, alert the school to demand action and then arrange a team of councillors for your traumatised son.

But when it's your son who's the bully, it's a different matter. Suddenly all the pity goes elsewhere. You can disown him as much as you like, tell people he takes after his mum, and ground him for life without parole, but it'll make no difference. You are tarnished as much as the bully himself. In fact, you may as well *be* the bully.

Whatever the scenario, you'll need to know how to deal with it. If your child is being picked on, he'll probably tell you, and you'll have to phone the other's boy's parents. If your kid is the baddie, then you'll receive the call.

Here's how they might go:

When *your* kid is being bullied

Brrr brrr
Gruff voice: Yeah?
You: Ah, hi there. Sorry to disturb you, but…
Gruff voice (now shouting): Shazza, turn tha' bloody music daan and shut the faacking dog up will yer I'm on the phone. Yeah, what?

You: Yep, I was calling in regards to you son, Lee

Gruff voice: Who? Oh 'im. We call 'im Nobby. What abaat it?

You: Well, it seems that he and my son, Malcolm have had a bit of a falling out, and…

Gruff voice: Oi, Shazza, I said shut the bleeding dog up before I break its faackin' neck. Give it one of them bones. What mate? Not bein' funny, but I'm watching Ice Road Truckers.

You: Yes, of course. It won't take a minute. You see Malcolm is very upset that Lee, er, Nobby has been a bit mean to him, and has been punching him in the…

Gruff voice: Wha you say? You callin' my lad a bully?

You: Oh, no, not at all. No no no, but he has been…

Gruff voice: Oi Shaz, a bloke here reckons Nobby's been giving his kid a kicking

Distant female voice (also gruff): My Lee's a good boy. He wouldn't do nun of tha'. Tell him to faak off.

Gruff voice: Who are yer any way? You wanna come raand here and sort it aat?

You: No, no, er, definitely not. I just wanted to see if there was any way you might ask Lee, er, Nobby if he could perhaps stop beating Malcolm up quite a often. And also give him back his inhaler.

Gruff voice: Look, mate. Not being' funny, but I ain't gunna let no bloke tell me 'ow to bring up my lad. If he needs a belting I'll give him one meself, awright?

You: Yes, I didn't man to…

Gruff voice: Well sling yer 'ook. I've a good mind to come raand there and give you a…

You: Er, no, that won't be necessary I can assure…. I'm very sorry to have called, er, thank you and I'm very sorry

Line goes dead

The important thing was you communicated the issue, made him realise the problem and reached a mutually agreeable solution. Most importantly you can tell your wife that you have dealt with it and that young Malcolm is safe to go back to school as soon as you've found him another one to go to.

Easy.

But what about the other way around?

When your kid is the *bully*

Brr brr

You: Hello?

Clipped voice: Good evening Mr Hartley, my name is Meddings and I'm calling in relation to your son, Malcolm

You: Oh, OK

Clipped voice: Your son has subjected my client's son to a sustained campaign of bullying over a period of time in excess of two months

You: Malcolm? Are you sure?

Clipped voice: Quite sure, Mr Hartley. As I'm sure you can appreciate, the boy concerned has been extremely traumatised by these events.

You: Well, I'm sorry to hear that. I will have a word with him, and…

Clipped voice: You will do much more than that, Mr Hartley. My client is a very patient man, but he feels that a financial recompense would be most appropriate to bring this matter to a close and to avoid any unnecessary judicial proceedings.

You: Judicial? You are joking, right?

Clipped voice: I never joke, Mr Hartley, especially not about such grave matters as these. We are also keen to avoid having to involve the police at this stage providing we can come to some agreement as to the level of punitive damage.

You: Just a minute. What exactly are you accusing my son of doing?

Clipped voice: I'm not accusing anyone of anything, Mr Hartley. I am merely acting on the instructions of my client who has the best interests of his son at heart. As a father yourself, I'm sure you understand.

You: Er, yes, I mean no. I mean how much do you want?

Clipped voice: I'm so glad you are being fair and reasonable about this, Mr Hartley. Court proceedings can be so unseemly… and expensive

You: Of course, of course. Please tell your client I am terribly sorry to hear about this and will urgently speak to Malcolm. What amount did you have in mind?

Clipped voice: My client will be asking for £25,000 including costs. The amount can be transferred via our bank account if that makes it easier?

You: Twenty…five… thousand? You cannot be serious

Clipped voice: I will understand, Mr Hartley if you prefer to have the matter dealt with by a magistrate and then a full sitting of a crown court. That is your absolute right. However, I must warn you that the legal fees alone are likely to be in excess of £25,000, perhaps double that amount.

You: Wha? Double? Look, I really don't want to… If you can give me your bank details, then…

Clipped voice: Of course, Mr Hartley. (gives account details)

You: Ok, Ok, I will transfer the money immediately. And do please accept my sincere apologies.

Clipped voice: I will indeed. I will call you back as soon as the money arrives. Good day.

Two hours later…
Brrr brrr
You: Hello

Clipped voice: Ah, Mr Hartley, just to inform you the money has been received. I am glad we've been able to resolve this unfortunate matter.

You: Yes, me too. Can I jut ask, what was it exactly that my son did to the other boy?

Clipped voice: The allegation is that your son called him, and I quote, a 'stupid prat'. Most damaging I'm sure you'd concur…

Again, the matter is dealt without any repercussions or recriminations and with the minimum amount of fuss. And a modest pecuniary payment is surely a small price to pay. Well, smallish.

If only we could be more straight with each other. Someone like Alf Stewart on Home and Away wouldn't pussyfoot around, would he? He'd get straight in, say what he had to say and then move on, possibly saying 'flaming galahs' at some point. Could your fateful call ever be like this?:

Brr brr
Bloke: Hello?
Alf: Mate, it's Alf. Yer boy's been whacking my kid. Tell him I'll brain him if he doesn't stop
Bloke: Fair dinkum. You wanna Fosters?
Alf: Yeah, alright.

The parents of bullied children aren't always so reasonable though. You may have to have a few lines ready for when you receive the call to make it less likely they will have your child expelled.

Excuses for your kid being a vicious, merciless bully include:

He's still grieving for his pet lobster
His ADHD is always worse when it's a full moon
He's been like this ever since the Tinky Winky misplaced his handbag
I probably gave him too much raw meat that morning

The doctor says it's actually really good that he can let his anger out like this

Well, I'm sure you'd be a bit upset too if you'd been anally probed by aliens

If it's any consolation, he hurt his knuckles when he punched your son the fifth time

He was disappointed that MENSA rejected him again

You son had a red shirt on? Ah, well that explains it.

He'd just had a playground argument about post neoclassical endogenous growth theory

Is there any way you could make your son more likeable?

Hey, what about girl bullies?

You are quite right that I have unfairly concentrated on boys, tarring them all with the same brutish brush, and ignored the possibility that girls can be bullies too.

Well, they can. And their form of bullying can be just as hurtful*.

For girls, the bullying is usually more verbal and less physical. True, there could be a few ponytails pulled, faces scratched and make-up smudged, but girls are the experts at what child psychologists call 'saying nasty things'.

To understand this better, you need to get inside the female psych, where everything is about appearances. It doesn't matter what something *does*, it's what it *looks like* that counts.

In adults this manifests itself in women wearing trendy, stylish yet uncomfortable shoes that give them blisters, lock knee and severe shin splints. If a man asks if it might not be wiser to wear shoes that fit, he will be ridiculed for his lack of understanding.

So, the young, female bully will be adept at knowing just how to make her victim feel like the world may as well end. ie attack her appearance.

---

* Though usually it involves fewer visible wounds and scars. If you don't count emotional scars.

Boys (and, let's face it, us blokes) don't really care about how we look unless we're on the pull, on trial or at a job interview. But girls do.

And if you're little girl is happily skipping off to school not realising that she's about to be subjected to a vile assault by one of her classmates, you're letting her down as a father.

Before you let her out of the house, go through this helpful, and potentially life-saving flowchart…

Is her school uniform too tight?
Yes – can you get a bigger size?
    Yes – Buy it now, you idiot
    No – Uh oh, then you need to work on her personality *
No – Continue to next question

Is her school uniform too short
Yes – make it longer before her morality is called into disrepute
No – Continue

Is it too long?
Yes – shorten it or else she'll be the daggy, frumpy no-friends nerdy drop out before recess
No – **Are you sure?**
    Yes - Continue
    No – actually, now you mention it, I've seen the Dowager Countess in Downton Abbey showing more skin

Is her hair plaited into pig tails?
No - Continue
Yes – Cut it all off now before her friends see! Actually, let's all calm down first. **Do any other girls have plaits?**
    Yes – **any cool girls?**
        Yes – Continue

* And probably her left hook

No, just one Rastafarian – thought not. Scissors out
No – Scissors out

Does she have any tasty treats in her lunchbox
Yes – good, at least the bullies might spare her once they've grabbed them
Does yogurt count? – No, they will smear it through her hair
No – Then she'll need cold, hard cash

Does she have red hair?
Yes – OK, then at least there will be no surprises
Is she trained in unarmed combat?
Yes – continue
No – then issue her with a knuckleduster to be safe
No – continue

Does she have pimples?
No – Continue
Yes – **Can they be disguised using make-up?**
Yes, possibly – continue
No, they're everywhere – **Do you have a mask she can wear?**
Yes – tell her she mustn't take it off under any circumstances
No – **Any bandages?**
Yes – Ok, apply them, you can say she was in a car crash or something
No – OK, well tell her the parable of the ugly ducking before she leaves the house

Is she wearing a brace?
Yes – tell her to keep her mouth closed
No – **Does she have hideous, wonky teeth?**

Oh yes, like tombstones – Ok, then the mouth stays shut
No – then she might just survive.

Phew! Looks like she's safe. For now. But be alert for telltale bruising and/or yogurt-streaked hair.

Homework

As a father you will from time to time be asked to help with your child's homework. This is fine when it's a six-year-old colouring in a drawing of a koala, but tricky when it's compound fractions, advanced chemistry or a critical evaluation of the role of Odysseus in Homer's Iliad.

To your little one, you are the font of all knowledge. No ones knows more than you about pretty much everything. To say that you don't know the answer to a question they are struggling with is akin to admitting you're a fraud, and will bring their little world crashing down around them, much like the city of Troy (which you'd know about if you'd bothered reading Homer's Iliad instead of watching Emmerdale).

So, assuming that there isn't time for you to bone up on the twelve years of schooling that you've forgotten, you need to bluff them into thinking that you're not a complete dunce.

When you are asked a question where you have absolutely no idea of the answer, try one of these lines to buy you some googling time…

That's a very important question. What was *your* first reaction?
I'd be very interested to hear what your mum thinks actually
She doesn't? Well, you know I'd be even more interested in Granny's opinion
Sure, I could tell you the answer, but let's make the most of the £5 donation I made to keep Wikipedia going
I would answer it right now, but the answer is pretty complicated and I promised your mum I'd give the dog his annual bath

Perhaps the better question is: why are they asking me this question?

As they say in Latin: 'verus scholasticus solves forsit su' – the true scholar works it out himself

It's quite easy actually. What you need to... oh, my phone's vibrating... oh lord, this is a very important call. You give your answer and I'll check it later... hello... hello?

Surviving exams

If school days are the best days of your life, then exam days are the worst days of the best days. And not being properly prepared means that your worst best days just got worse still.

As a father, you want your kids to do well at school so they can fulfil their potential, realise their goals, succeed in their chosen career and one day buy you that sports car you always wanted.

A kid who flunks out, is a kid who'll be living under your roof and eating your food a whole lot longer than is natural. Even humpback whales find their own digs eventually.

So you need them to do well in whatever test they are taking, be it end of year exams, A levels, college degree or remedial certificate in concrete mixing.

But how? If they're not the sharpest knives in the drawer, it's not going to be easy.*

Here's how:

1. Manage expectations

If there's more chance of a Jim'll Fix It rerun than little Felicita getting straight As, concentrate instead on achieving at least something. Maybe if she spent less time revising a no hope subject like physics, and more on food science, it might bear some fruit**.

* Especially if they drawer doesn't even contain any more knives
** Literally, when they learn to make apple pie

2. Absolve yourself of all responsibility

This is a step you don't actually acknowledge (for obvious reasons*) but will make things a lot less stressful for you. Gently direct all exam-related issues to your wife so that she can take charge and bear the brunt. You can be there too, but in a more honorary basis.

3. Offer some profound words of encouragement.

And if you can't actually think of anything profound, quote a famous person.

Something like this:

Every day you may make progress. Every step may be fruitful. Yet there will stretch out before you an ever-lengthening, ever-ascending, ever-improving path. You know you will never get to the end of the journey. But this, so far from discouraging, only adds to the joy and glory of the climb.
~ Sir Winston Churchill

Not quite sure what the old boy was getting at, but it sounds like it might be confidence boosting. And how about this one:

"You may never know what results come of your action, but if you do nothing there will be no result."
~ Mahatma Gandhi

Hmm. Again, there appears to be a very meaningful thought there, and something about doing things being better than not doing them. Which is definitely true**.

* They're not obvious? Hmm, I hope your father managed *your* expectations
** Unless the 'things' are bad things, in which case it's generally better *not* to do them

4. Don't let them see that you're at all worried

Because if you do, it'll make them worried. And then you'll be worried that they're worried you're worried because you are worrying about this damn exam. Instead, be nonchalant, wish them good luck and then pray to whatever God will listen and offer up your soul for a decent result.

Coping with failure

It doesn't matter how well you prepare them, or how many times you quote Gandhi, there is still a chance that they won't get the result they were hoping for.

They will open the results envelope and see all their dreams of being rocket scientists, design engineers, marine biologists or giraffe proctologists disappear in an instant.

This is when they need their dad the most. Not just for a manly hug (or a less manly one if it's your daughter) and a few platitudes, but for some reassurance that they can still make less of a hash of their life than you did.

So, here's how:

1. Famous people who were high school drop outs

Richard Branson, Bill Gates, Thomas Eddison, Albert Einstein, Walt Disney, Ned Kelly, er, Princess Diana. Of course, strictly speaking, there are millions of high school drop outs who aren't actually famous, mainly because they were high school drop outs, but let's leave that aside for now.

2. They still have their health

This one sounds (and is) a bit desperate, but it's worth pointing out. If they *don't* actually have their health, then you could still touch on it by listing all the disabilities they *don't* have. Or you could skip to point three.

3. They can try again

One defeat doesn't mean the season's over* so let's dust ourselves off and realise that this failure isn't the end - it could be the first of many. And there's every chance that if you keep plugging away, the law of averages means something good will happen eventually. When you tell them this, you may want to reword it to make it clearer.

4. We're still very proud of you

Why? You really have to ask? Well, for a start you did your best, kind of, and that counts for something. And you didn't give up until you absolutely had to give up, which took real, er, patience. And even then you were a good loser – not that were saying you lost, just that you didn't quite win, or indeed draw. Also, you're so…so, er, tall. We've always been proud of your height.

5. Money and success don't buy happiness

There are legions of very successful people who have ended up topping themselves because they were so unhappy. It's really very lucky that you didn't pass because we'd hate you to get like that. Abject poverty is good for the soul. And, no, you can't borrow ten bucks for some smokes.

6. Tomorrow is another day

If all else fails, just parrot a few meaningless clichés to them until they snap out of it and pull themselves together. Stuff like:

> What will be will be
> Every road has its bumps
> It's always darkest before the dawn
> God works in mysterious ways
> Always look on the bright side
> We've all been to the school of hard knocks
> It'll all come out in the wash

* Except, occasionally, for Grimsby Town

Not choosing bad subjects

As they get older, school students are unwisely given the opportunity to have some say in their own education. This ludicrous idea makes them think that it's up to them what subjects they choose to study and what career path these may lead to.

This notion needs to be stamped out. As their father, you are far better placed to decide what is best for them, though making *them* see this can be a challenge.

Kids in years Seven, Eight and Nine are motivated by two things: laziness and fear of hard work. So these two factors help determine their choices.

You may want them to choose chemistry, English literature and engineering, but there's a danger they'll veer instead towards sports science, woodwork and catering

Not that there's anything wrong with these subjects – especially if they need to fashion a hockey stick and do the half time refreshments – but are they being chosen for the right reasons?

If you suspect they aren't then, you need to subtly step in and guide them so they have no idea they are being guided. Simply imply it's nerdy, hard work, involves hours of homework every night and is taught by a flatulent grump nicknamed Severus Snape.

8

Help! They're getting bigger!

*"I'm not going to buy my kids an encyclopedia.
Let them walk to school like I did."*
~ ***Yogi Berra***

"My parents have been there for me ever since I was about seven"
~ ***David Beckham***

Just like debts and tomato plants, children tend to grow over time. Unlike tomato plants, however, they can have issues that cannot be contained to a green house or terracotta pot.

Very small children are simple enough because they are just that: simple. You just need to feed, de-soil and feign an interest in Bob the Builder. Job done. It's a bit like having a virtual pet, but with a bit more guilt if it dies of neglect.

Since they have no control over their lives, you can point them in roughly the right direction and then stick plasters on their grazed knees.

At the time, it didn't seem at all easy, but compared to older kids approaching their teenage years they were a doddle.

As your sons and daughters develop their own minds, there are many more things that can (and will) go wrong. If, that is, you're not prepared. And that's where this chapter comes in.

In truth, it's a bit of a jumbled collection of thoughts, that didn't really fit anywhere else in the book, spuriously tied together.

That said, it still contains vital advice no father in his right mind should be without.

We start with a moral dilemma...

Should you lie to your children?

Lying is an invaluable skill for fathers. Not just lying, but lying *well*. Anyone who thinks that children should always be told the truth no matter what, has either never had kids, still believes in Santa or has incurred a serious brain injury.

The ability to lie is what separates us from the animals* and is the very fabric that holds our society together. If God had had a bigger stone tablet to play with, 'Thou shalt lie to younger generations at every opportunity' would have been the eleventh commandment.

Still not convinced? Didn't Jim Carrey's Liar Liar teach you *anything*? Apart from the dangers of a Hollywood actor basing a career on one facial expression.

Well, by all means try being truthful if it makes you feel better about yourself. I'll give you twenty-four hours before a police appointed child care professional is dispatched to your house.

Lying is an art form right up there with oil painting and synchronised swimming, but you need to be able to separate the 'good lies' from the 'bad truths'.

This can take time and, as you don't have the luxury of time, let's skip through it quickly. If you have any questions, wait until the end...

Good lie: Father Christmas is going to give you presents if you've been a good girl.

* That and moist toilet tissue

Bad truth: an old, overweight man is going to enter your room while you're asleep and empty his sack next to your bed.

Good lie: Your mum and dad love you every second of every day.
Bad truth: ...but your adoptive parents sold you to feed their crystal meth habit.

Good lie: I don't care what anyone says, you're a very clever boy.
Bad truth: ... but don't worry so much about business studies and maths, just concentrate in woodwork.

Good lie: I'm afraid little Fluffy has run away to the wild.
Bad truth: Well, yes, that *might* be fur in the dog's poo...

Good lie: No, we don't have enough money for an ice cream.
Bad truth: It's not my fifth beer, it's only the fourth.

Good lie: Mummy and Daddy won't be living together anymore, but we still love you and we'll always be friends
Bad truth: ...but if anyone mentions the plumber's name in the house again, I will flush their head round the U-bend.

Good lie: Hey, don't cry, winning isn't everything. I'm sure you did your best
Bad truth: Hey, don't cry, you'll soon get used to losing if that's the best you can do.

As children get older, they will realise that you have lied to them about almost everything. The Tooth Fairy, Easter Bunny, why Mummy was screaming in bed and that the music played by a Mr Whippy van *doesn't* mean that it's run out of ice cream.

They won't hate you for this (after all £2 for a tooth that ends up in the bin isn't bad) but they will be less trusting. Hence the need to lie in a believable way and hope they haven't got access to a phonograph machine.

To look more sincere, simply use the soon-to-be-patented Bullshit method:

Be confident – don't speak it, *announce* it.
Use their name – saying: 'Mia, I know you think that it was me who broke wind, but it was definitely the dog.'
Look 'em in the eye – glancing sideways makes you look shifty
Leave out the pleading – avoid phrases like 'you must believe me', 'for the love of God it's the truth' and 'I'm begging you, please just accept it and don't tell your mother'.
Supporting evidence – eg 'I think a cursory glance at the works of Yung will make it clear that it is actually perfectly possible that when I took your pocket money, I was acting sub-consciously.
Hark back to previous conversations – 'Have I ever lied to you before? Huh? Oh yeah, but I meant *apart* from those times.'
Invoke The Bible – 'As Jesus taught us, there are some things that cannot be explained away by mere facts. You need to have *faith* that I don't have £5 in my wallet for another Sprite.'
Try not to threaten – you don't need to resort to stuff like 'If you don't say you believe me, so help me I will cane your bottom into a meat patty.'

Stick this list up on the fridge if you think you might forget some of them. But if one of the kids spots it, say you've never seen it before. If he believes you, then give yourself a pat on the back.

However, there is another side to this – being lied *to*.
This is a very serious matter – if you catch your *child* telling a fib, unleash hell.
Tell them that you will never tolerate lying in your household, that you can never trust them again, they are a disgrace to the family name and

that you have never told a lie in your life. Add in something sanctimonious about the boy who cried wolf, George Washington cutting down the cherry tree and Kim Kardashian's wedding vows for good effect.

The punishment will depend on their age:

3-6 years: The Naughty Step. But make them understand that it's not the step itself that is naughty.
7-12 years: No TV for a week! Or at least until you forget that you banned it.
13-16 years: Foot rub for Great Aunt Myrtle
17-18 years: Confiscate their marijuana and say you're going to tell Santa

Mother's Day

Until now you've given your old mum a box of Cadbury's Favourites, a card and maybe invited her over for lunch. Job done.

But now that's all changed. You now have a mother in your immediate family. And it's not her children who have to spoil her on her big day. Oh no, they're too selfish and lazy and will use the excuse that they are a 'baby' to avoid making breakfast in bed and signing a card.

So it's left to you to have to roll out the red carpet for *two* mums*.

As a rule of thumb, this is what's expected:

Her first Mother's Day: Full cooked breakfast in bed with champagne, fancy card, scented candle, flower arrangement, perfume, whisked off for lunch at expensive restaurant followed by bubble bath with scattered rose petals and more champagne.

The next one: The same but the flowers are from a BP service station, and the candle smells vaguely of detergent.

* Or even three if you have a demanding granny too

After that: Cup of tea in bed after several kicks in the groin, Cadbury's Favourites, card, you stick a pizza in the oven for lunch

When the kids reach school age, they will bring home a crude, handmade card from school, but it'll still be you who does the hard yards. Only when they get to about ten will they consent to perhaps making the tea – but you'll still need to get out of your nice warm bed to remind them, supervise, and then do it yourself when it goes wrong or they lose interest.

Father's Day

On the upside, now you're a dad, you are entitled to be pampered too. This will consist of your wife throwing a card at you and telling the kids that 'This is Daddy's special day'. An hour later she'll remind you that the guttering still hasn't been cleared out and the dog isn't going to walk itself.

Your present will be one of the following, none of which will ever see the light of day.

A gaudy tie
Old fashioned shaving kit
A tool you already have
Your wife's favourite chocolate
Whisky blended in a Japanese prison
Novelty socks
Personalised mug
Ear and nose hair trimmer
Box of checked handkerchiefs
'Amusing book' which takes five minutes to read*
600-page novel by an author your wife thinks you should like

* And before you say anything, this one takes at least fifteen

Rake
Deadliest Catch boxset
Bottle of extra hot chili sauce
Singing trout to mount on the wall
A manbag
Useless desktop gadget
Football-themed cufflinks
Hair loss products
Mobile phone belt holster
A potty putter for use while defecating
BBQ apron expressing your fondness for beef
REO Speedwagon's greatest hits
An aftershave your youngest picked up at the school fete.
Floor mats for the car

Is your child depressed?

Kids don't have mortgages, stressful jobs, nagging wives, unruly offspring, back problems, male pattern baldness, long term unemployment, alcoholism or credit card debts so you'd think their lives would be one long holiday. And they don't even have to pay for the holiday.

But, despite all this, studies show that more and more of them suffer from depression. There are two things to take from this fact: a) you need to be attuned to possible symptoms, and b) as it's so widespread, it can't *just* be your bad fathering.

But how do you tell if a child is really unhappy or just faking it so you buy her another slice of cherry pie to cheer her up.*

To take the worry out of worrying about your child worrying, simply look for these indicators that you might need to be worried…

* Which could be counter productive if she's depressed about being overweight

7 Tell-tale signs your daughter is depressed
1. Cut marks on arms of Barbie doll
2. Leonard Cohen album on her ipod
3. Wears a 'Forever 7' T-shirt days before her 8th birthday
4. Sits on her bed, swiveling head, in a pool of pea soup
5. Requests a Titanic-themed birthday party.
6. Asks if you can buy real gas for dolls house oven
7. Downloads theme to Vera Drake as ringtone

7 Tell-tale signs your son is depressed
1. Lies motionless across Thomas the Tank Engine train track
2. Demands padding on bedroom walls.
3. Asks Gramps his views on suicide pacts.
4. GI Joe found beneath pillow
5. Has Childline on speed dial
6. Writes to Santa asking for a cyanide capsule
7. Graduates straight from Dr Seuss to 'We Need to Talk About Kevin'.

If you now think that one of the kids might be so inclined, you should do what all good fathers do, and murmur a series of glib comments. Here are a few failsafe ones to get you going…

> Cheer up son, no point in dwelling
> It'll be all right in the end
> Come on, I'll buy you a lolly
> Stiff upper lip, now
> Pull yourself together and you'll be fine
> Haaaay, is that a smile I see? Is it? *Is it?*
> Why don't you have a chat with your mother

Ok, so we've hopefully got them over their depression. If you think they may still be a bit down, try a more forceful approach by telling them to man up (especially if it's a girl) and remind them that there are millions of people worse off than them in the world*. Also throw in that Stephen Fry is clinically depressed, and he always seems happy enough. Case closed. Quod erat demonstratum, as they say.

How to make sure they're not nerds

All fathers start off naively thinking they can control their kid's personality as they grow and thereby produce a son or daughter in their own image, or, better still, in the image of someone smarter and slimmer. You figure that the toys you buy them, the parenting methods you employ, the discipline you use and the behaviour-altering drugs you force down their throats will all have the desired effect.

Well they won't. If they did, Mr and Mrs Assange wouldn't be in such a fix with young Julian.

No, try as you might, your kids will be nothing like the children you hoped they would.

The tip here is to have extremely low expectations so there's a small chance they'll be exceeded.

There are several ways children can go wrong, but the one we need to speak of here is that of the nerd.

The dictionary defines such a person thus: 'An intelligent but socially inept, physically awkward person, usually obsessed by non-social activities. Prone to introversion and unattractiveness.'

In other words, he's not going to captain the school's rugby team. And if it's a girl, she won't be first pick on prom night.

* However, if you're reading this in a Mumbai slum with only grilled sewer rat for lunch, leave that last observation out. Or say there are 'probably a few people' worse off.

There are those who would rather their children turn out in *any* other way than be a nerd, but this is cruel*. Surely it's better to have a nerd than a, oh, let's say a serial killer, isn't it?

Let's see:

Is it better to bring up a serial killer or a nerd?

Advantages of serial killer
Doesn't have to worry about his pension
You can sell his baby photos to The Daily Star
…and flog your story to Channel 5.
Ready made anecdotes for boring dinner parties
He won't make you engage in role playing fantasy games
If he got away with several killings before being apprehended, it at least shows some initiative
Dissolving bodies in the bath suggests he *was* paying attention in chemistry
He isn't an embarrassing nerd

Advantages of nerd
Less likely to bury bodies in your back garden.
Can show you how to download pirated movies
He gets a bit less pity now that The Big Bang Theory is popular
You won't get dragged along to loads of boring school sports days
Less chance of being cornered by an irate father demanding you pay for his daughter's abortion
Won't start thrashing you at tennis before puberty
Marginally more hope of getting grandchildren than if he were a mass murderer sentenced to life in solitary confinement.
Wouldn't have the physical strength to murder anyone

* Understandable, but still cruel

Well, I think at best, that's inconclusive. Worst case scenario is a serial killing nerd, but, in practice, it's probably wiser to do all you can to avoid both outcomes.

Can you make them less nerdy?

Simple – just follow this five step plan:

1. Books are your enemy
No one wants to see their kids reading about life when they could be experiencing it. Tell them to get outside, kick a ball around, climb a tree or go trout fishing. Books are for the bookish.

2. Enough with the science!
Yes, scientists have given us penicillin, rudimentary robots and the Large Hadron Collider, but do you really want your daughter to wear a white lab coat, thick-rimmed glasses and drone on about protons? Of course not. As you've put so much effort into raising them, time last thing you want is boring adults kids who can't even entertain you.

3. Let's get physical
Nerds have the upper body strength of a stick insect, so you're going to need to show them the benefits of getting out of breath occasionally. We're not talking iron man events here, merely a little exercise now and then. Perhaps make them walk to the library to get their geeky books or put them on a treadmill when they're playing online Minecraft or Battlefield Hero. If all else fails, give them protein shakes and steroids to give them a small chance of impress women with their muscles.

4. Popular culture
You're in charge of their TV viewing, so blocking channels like BBC Knowledge, National Geographic and Discovery Science can

give you the opportunity to introduce them to character building TV shows like Family Guy, Jersey Shore and TOWIE - shows they can discuss with their cool friends thereby making them popular.

5. Look more jock-like
This bit's easy – more hoodies, white sneakers and footy tops, fewer buttoned-up checked shirts, bow ties, curly hair, round spectacles and buck teeth.

Ok, so the five step plan turned out to have six points, but only a nerd would notice that, so we'll move on.

Imaginary friends
In Hollywood movies, these can be creepy and even homicidal, but in reality this is uncommon. Only a small minority tell their humans to kill and maim, and even then it's rarely the dad who gets hurt. Usually it's a girlfriend, boyfriend or teacher so you're pretty safe.

An imaginary friend usually starts between the ages or four and six and can either go on for just a couple of years or hang around into those already difficult teen years.

If you have a very young child with one, then that's good for you – they can keep each other entertained while you wash the car or read the paper.

Problems arise when the kid is older and spending so much time with a fictional mate that they don't have any time for real ones. And people can be very cruel about kids who talk into thin air.

So overall, are they a good thing or a bad thing? Let's see:

Good: Cheaper to take to Macca's
Bad: Blames her for the empty cookie jar

Good: Less likely to kick a football through your window.

Bad: Probably has a fictional father more impressive than you

Good: Causes trauma if your child's imaginary friend starts playing with another kid
Bad: Birthday parties less fun if none of the guests are real

Good: Imaginary friend isn't going to teach your kid swear words
Bad: Upsetting if your kid is dumped by his imaginary friend because he doesn't believe your kid exists

Are you ready to answer all their questions?

Children instinctively know to which parent they need to go to ask different questions. After all, as a father, you can't be expected to know *everything* about *everything all* the time, can you? Or even *some* of the time, if we're honest. So it may be helpful to illustrate this so you'll understand what to expect...

Questions they ask Mum
What's for breakfast?
Where's my school bag?
Can I go to Chloe's after school?
When is rugby?
When is my homework due?
Where are my pajamas?
What can I have to eat?
How do I top up my phone?
How much is the museum trip?
Where is my tennis racquet?
How do you spell 'Grandma'?
What time is my trumpet lesson?
Do you have a Band Aid?
Am I allowed to play on the Xbox?
Is it PE today?

When is the dentist?
Who's picking me up from the party?
Is that old man *really* my uncle?
Is my sports kit washed?

Questions they ask Dad
Where's Mum?

Christmas

"It was the best of times, it was the worst of times" as whatshisface once said about something. But they could have been talking about Christmas for a father.

Yes, you get presents, eat mince pies and get to show off your charades prowess, but the festive season will also be one of the most stressful, thankless and exhausting times of the year – right up there with your mother-in-law's annual toga and tarts party.

For a start, Christmas costs money. Lots of money. And your kids won't thank you for coughing up all your hard earned cash, oh no – they'll take it for granted. And, worse, Father Flippin' Christmas will get all the credit.

As with most aspects of fatherhood, your success will depend on two things: a) preparation and b) alcohol.

Actually, there may be a 'c)' here as well which is: avoiding blame for things that are clearly your fault. Because from the moment you get the decorations out of the garage to the time, the non-broken ones get shoved back in, there are just so many traps to fall into.

So, preparation. Here is your checklist:

1. You have bought some really nice red and white wine, plus a few £1.99 bottles from Oddbins for when the in-laws turn up and stick a straw in the top.

2. You have also hidden the bottle of 40-year-old French Courvoisier so your wife doesn't pour it on the Christmas pud.
3. You have enough wrapping paper to comfortably conceal a Sherman tank
4. You've managed to steal a jewellery box from that expensive store into which the Elizabeth Duke earrings have been placed.
5. The Sunday supplements containing the gadgets and clothes you'd like bought for you have been left around the sitting room, and several other rooms
6. You've bought batteries for all the electronic kids' presents. Plus that thing the wife wanted after reading 50 Shades.
7. You've got back up batteries for Aunt Glenda's hearing aid to avoid another unseemly row during charades.
8. If you have very small children, you have a high shelf ready for any nice presents they receive which can be re-gifted at all the birthday parties they goes to.
9. The fire extinguisher is within easier reach than last year for setting light to the pudding.
10. You've scraped the dried smears of pig blood off your apron that has the amusing breasts on the front.
11. You've got the USB stick with last year's Queen's Speech on to placate Granny when you forget to watch it this year.

Ok, so you're prepared. Nothing can go wrong, now right? If you'd like to believe this, then don't say I didn't warn you when suddenly it's Christmas morning and panic has set in.

You see, Christmas Day itself is like a food drop at a Sudanese refugee camp. The beautifully wrapped pile of presents under the tree will be lovingly opened the way lawn mower processes grass.

No child will remember which present was given by which aunt, so you've no idea how to word the thank you note. This will be your fault as Mummy is too busy spending seven hours preparing lunch.

The first fight will break out after about present opening number three. One child will notice that another got something they didn't. This will result in a declaration of war. Not kid vs kid, but kid vs you. It is your fault that Christmas has been ruined.

Even two gifts molecularly identical in every way except colour can be the trigger. All it will take is for one child to look at both items and declare: 'Yes! I got the yellow one!'

This will cause both your wife and mother to tutt, roll their eyes at each other and exchange looks that indicate that they would never have made the same schoolboy mistake.

So, to avoid further calamity, cut out this list of mistakes you could (and probably will) make and stick it to your forehead, or better still, someone else's so you can actually read it.

You put too much brandy in the brandy butter so no one will eat it, except for the toddler who's on his way to casualty to have his stomach pumped

You didn't react will sufficient excitement and joy after unwrapping eau de David Beckham

You should have checked the fairy lights worked before spending two hours untangling them

A female condom isn't a suitable present for your teenage niece

Your four-year-old might actually still believe in Santa if he hadn't seen him slumped asleep still clutching the half-stuffed stocking and a empty Budweiser bottle in the early hours of Christmas morning.

Your actions under the mistletoe with cousin Fran technically constitute a sexual assault

Complaining about being given metallic green Shrek pajamas is unreasonable as you'd said you 'didn't mind' what sort you got.

Interpreting your wife saying 'we don't need to get each other presents this year, do we?' as meaning she doesn't expect a present from you this year was naïve and selfish.

Not realising Granddad was having a heart attack during charades, and guessing 'Hearts in Atlantis' was callous.

After your 'tidy up', it becomes apparent that the front row tickets for the Old Trafford game that your dad gave you must be in one of the fourteen bin liners full of screwed up wrapping paper.

You should have remembered that your great grandmother has a new hip before goading her into a snowball fight.

As no one found your Michael Caine and Dame Edna impressions funny last year, why did you feel the need to repeat them?

Yes, you live under the same roof, see each other nearly every minute of every day and you tell her that you love her at least ten times a day, but that doesn't mean you didn't need to spend £8 on a posh Christmas card to tell her how much you love her.

It was your decision, and your decision alone to buy the kids chocolate advent calendars and should have foreseen that no doors would remain unopened by December 2nd.

Giving the middle child a calculator so she could add up the monetary value of her presents and those of her siblings, was always going to end badly.

Your reflection to the priest at Midnight Mass that it's sad that Christmas just isn't as commercial as it used to be and 'Did Santa die on the cross for nothing?' was bound to offend him.

Should you become a househusband?

Just think – no office politics, commuting, being passed over for promotion, working lunches or stress. All you have to do is drop the kids at school and maybe walk the dog or take a nap before picking them up again at 3pm. Bung a pizza in the oven, stick on some washing and grab a cold beer before the missus gets home all frazzled at 6pm.

The only problem might be finding stuff to occupy all those long, empty hours.

Yep, this is surely a no-brainer – you even get to bond with your adorable children, spend quality time with them, and watch Judge Judy.

But before you tell the boss where to stick his snow scene paperweight, we need a reality check here. You're getting carried away in a fantasy world because, and I'm whispering this, it turns out that being the primary care provider isn't the bed of roses you might have thought. Yes, if you are seriously considering going all daddy day care, then consider these ten mistakes that nearly all househusbands make when adjusting to their new status…

Thinking you can handle the loss of status

Ok, so you won't miss getting home shattered to find only the dog's pleased to see you, but at least you'd spent the day engaging with other adults, albeit some of them dumber than your kids. You had important decisions to make, were respected by your workmates and lunched at a trendy restaurant where the napkins weren't made of paper. Now the important decisions will involve whether your youngest is more likely to eat Ben 10 or Monsters Inc yoghurt (probably he'll go ape-shit because you didn't buy Transformers 'No Bits' fromage frais) and if you can get away with giving him the bolognaise sauce which has sat fizzing in the fridge for a week.

However, if you, in fact, had no status, garnered no respect from your colleagues and lunched standing up at KFC, then this point shouldn't concern you.

Hoping your kids won't notice your 'little cock ups'

There are some errors you will only make once – putting uncooked bacon in packed lunches, thinking it was ham, and mistaking the antibacterial wipes containing bleach for moist toilet tissue while administering to your toddler. With each understandable mishap, you'll see a look in their eye, which says 'Mummy wouldn't have done that'. Then Mummy will get home, be informed and confirm that she has indeed never done that.

At least at work, if you cocked up, the only consequences were your company losing money, a furious client, a newly built house collapsing or a patient dying. And for each, the blame is a lot easier to shift.

Dusting off the golf clubs
Once you've tidied away the breakfast dishes and completed the school run, there's surely a nice round of golf-sized hole in your day before the afternoon pick up?

Sadly your golf clubs will soon have a fresh coat of dust on them, as it turns out that the six hours between 9am and 3pm get sucked into a time warp and actually last about an hour. And that's *with* all your crafty time saving measures such as taking dirty clothes out of laundry baskets, refolding them and stuffing them into the kids' drawers.

Yes, but then how do women find time for all those coffee mornings, clothes shopping, manicures and games of tennis? I'm glad you've raised that because this is at the root of the whole misconception about how easy it is to be a housewife. The answer is simple – they practise it from the moment they learn to stand upright and push their dolly around in a pram.

After so many years when you're happily not paying attention, they become fully qualified experts and can do the same amount of work in less than half the time.

Of course, most won't admit this little secret as it will mean you will pity their hard graft (even) less than you do now. By the time, you've had enough time to hone your housework/child rearing skills, said children will have their own children.

Not following washing machine instructions

During your first week of being in charge, it will be brought to your attention that there is a white, metal machine that sits in that little room between the kitchen and the door to the patio. Funny how you never noticed it before really.

Your wife will talk you through how it works, but you won't be paying attention because, hey, why should you? It cleans clothes – big deal!

After your first couple of attempts, you'll wonder what prompted your wife to buy so many pale pink items (including underwear for you apparently) and why on earth you have a cashmere sweater small enough for a Barbie doll.

One error you will only make once is not checking pockets for sticks of stringy cheese, dirty tissues, half-eaten sandwiches and pet frogs, and then, having washed all the clothes, shoving them into the tumble dryer. The resulting aroma will be far from the 'summer meadow' promised on the washing powder box. Newly abandoned slaughterhouse will be closer to the mark.

Also in that first week, one of your ungrateful kids will ask you over breakfast (in front of your wife) where their school shirt is. As you remember that you left it dripping wet inside the washing machine, one delightfully sneaky idea will occur – the microwave. If it can warm up cold coffee and defrost fish fingers, it can surely dry a simple cotton shirt.

Well, yes it can. As well as turning it a crispy brown colour that would look great on a pizza, but is less appetising now. The best thing now is to quietly dispose of it and then blame the kid for losing 'yet another' item of their uniform.*

Getting caught up in school gate politics

Far from being a happy place where children skip out of class into the arms of their adoring mothers, who are all having a bit of a giggle with each other, the school gate is a seething tangle of warring gangs and rival tribes, all of whom will immediately be suspicious that a man has entered their midst.

---

* After the zip-up fleece that caught fire when you hung it over the toaster last week.

If you chat to one, you'll be blanked by others because her little boy hit their little girl.

Also there will be be:

a) The tarty single mum with the short, denim skirt and big, hoop earrings who the others resent for looking like a hooker. Her daughter will typically be named after a Spice Girl or Pussycat Doll.

b) The severe-looking shouty matron whose volume level is permanently set at 'Festival speaker'.

c) The bitchy gossip who gleefully spreads destructive rumours about any mum not present at that precise moment.

d) The dishevelled dad, slumped against a wall staring into the middle distance who's either long term unemployed, recently divorced or on parole.

e) The plump Earth Mother who wears several shades of brown, has rosy cheeks and smiles vacantly the whole time. She'll also hand out her homemade beetroot chutney.

They all get on about as well as Japanese fighting fish in a jam jar. The best advice is to hover at the edge of the playground, quietly beckon the kids over, bundle them into he car and speed off without a sideways glance.

Cooking healthy food

As the old proverb probably doesn't go: you can lead children to chopped up carrots with a hummus dip, but you can't make them eat it. Yes, porridge doesn't need honey if it contains chopped up bananas and sultanas, but your children know that if they stage a hunger strike for long enough, you will crack long before Mummy ever would. And once you've given in, there is no going back and black, rotten teeth will follow. It then becomes a case of making sure the Domino's boxes are buried deep in the recycling bin and that a few strands of carrot peel are placed next to the sink for effect before Mummy gets back from work. Don't worry – you won't be grassed up as your co-conspirators have too much to lose if their mother finds out.

Imagining it will buy you sex

A recent study found that women who work full time and then have housework to do are too tired for sex. With this knowledge front of mind, you will put on and hang out two loads of washing, vacuum and dust upstairs and down, cook the kids' tea, get the shopping in and clean the kitchen until its germ levels are those of a special care baby unit. There will be *nothing* left for your wife to do. By the time she gets home from work, however, you'll be asleep on the sofa and won't stir until morning.

Volunteering at the school

This will come about when a friendly mum asks you if you might be able to help out with some classroom reading. When no excuse comes to mind quickly enough and you agree, you will find yourself firstly conscripted as a classroom assistant and then put in charge of the Christmas fete and fund raising auction, coopted onto the parent council, becoming coach of the under sevens rounders team and then assigned lollipop lady duty outside the school twice a week for a minimum of four years. Your reward will be a small footnote of thanks on one of the weekly school newsletters. You will be hated even more by all the mums for showing them up.

Expecting your mates to treat you the same

Until you give up work, you will have no idea how much of your conversation with mates down the pub is about, well, work. From stories of pissed colleagues and deals gone awry to the hot new girl in sales and that huge account you just won against astronomical odds. The one rule is: you don't talk about your kids because that's boring. But that *is* your job now. Which makes you boring. Also, your job defines who you are. eg 'This is Peter, he's an architect.' Now for you it will be: 'This is Adam, he cleans the toilet and irons his wife's skirts (badly).'

Waiting for a few words of thanks

When you work, you get paid money. If you do something good, people thank you, and from time to time you might even be promoted and given a shiny new title.

Now, you are putting in longer hours and working directly with the 'clients', but your work is invisible. On the (probably rare) occasions you slave for hours over a hot kitchen to whip up a delicious dinner, the kids will begrudgingly pick at it for a bit and then ask if there is 'anything else'. No one will notice the swept floors, fresh linen or clean oven… just as *you* had never noticed them in the past.

9

Teenagers

"We live in a society of laws. Why do you think I took you to all those Police Academy movies? For <u>fun</u>? Well, I didn't hear anybody laughing, did you?"

"I'm trying to be a sensitive father, you unwanted moron!"
~ ***Homer Simpson***

As Forrest Gump nearly said, 'teenagers are like a box of chocolates – you never know what you're going to get next'.

What he would have meant had he said this is that when a child turns thirteen, chemical reactions inside their body mean that they become what child psychologists call 'unpredictable'. And a bit unhinged.

This can be disconcerting to a doting father such as yourself who has spent the last thirteen years nurturing a child genius/sporting prodigy/future reality TV star, and now finds all their good work undone.

How can this have happened? When *you* were thirteen, you weren't like this – you were respectful, God-fearing and enchanted by Bagpuss and Danger Mouse.

But this pimple-plagued, gum-chewing lump of angst sprawled over your sofa listening to Florence and the Machine while sexting a girl in his class and staring blankly at Channel V is barely the same species. Is evolution going backwards?

Well, no. And yes.

Teenagers today are indeed more slouched, mono syllabic and fat, but on the plus side* they are too lazy and exhausted to rebel against authority like you used to.

And, to further complicate matters, teenagers can become teenage before their teenage years. Yes – it is possible to have a teenager before you have a thirteen-year-old. Puberty is happening sooner in boys and girls, so you need to highly attuned to the warning signs. And conversely, maybe that sixteen-year-old hasn't yet gone through 'the change' and you've been worrying needlessly.

Take this little test to confirm once and for all whether your child has reached their teenage years.

1. You walk through the front door after work to be greeted by:
a) Daddy! You're home!
b) Silence

2. At their birthday party you spend most of the time:
a) Supervising the musical bumps and piñata.
b) On the door checking IDs

3. A red, cratered landscape with frequent eruptions best describes:
a) The picture of Mount Doom on their wall
b) Their face

4. The thing they do most on the PC is:
a) Their history homework
b) Clicking on 'Delete history'

5. You give them homework if they:
a) Do their chores
b) Agree to sit at the other end of the sofa until they've had a shower

* Or, more accurately, plus *size*

6. If you hear furtive sounds coming from their bedroom at night, you:
a) Tell them to stop playing Lego
b) Knock first

7. When you pick them up from a party, you:
a) Make sure they have their party bag and all of their fairy princess costume
b) Put plastic sheeting on their car seats and bring a sick bag

8. Their bedroom has the aroma of:
a) Freshly laundered linen
b) A Turkish wrestler's jock strap

9. Before they drift off to sleep, they love to:
a) Read a few pages of Diary of a Wimpy Kid
b) Quickly finish the assignment that was due in three days ago.

10. As the weeks pass, the change you notice most is:
a) They've got even more cute-as-a-button freckles
b) Your single malt tastes a little watered down

11. When they speak they sound:
a) Excited at being alive
b) Less erudite than a Cro-Magnon cave dweller

12. On Sunday morning, he:
a) Still accompanies you to church
b) Plays with a different organ

Mostly As

Your child has precisely no active testosterone or estrogen, believes in the Easter Bunny and frankly sounds a little irritating. But he or she is not a teenager so you can breathe easy. However, take this test every single week from now on because the situation can change literally overnight*

Mostly Bs

Your child has more hormones than meat processing plant. Prepare for that first training bra or for balls to drop like cherries from a tree, and don't say I didn't warn you.

Being a father to a teenager is not something you can avoid unless your kid is Peter Pan - and even he abandoned the Lost Boys for a girl. So instead, embrace it and do your best to understand what they are going through.

Teenage angst

Urbandictionary.com defines angst as:

"A transcendent emotion in that it combines the unbearable anguish of life with the hopes of overcoming this seemingly impossible situation. Without the important element of hope, then the emotion is anxiety, not angst. Angst denotes the constant struggle one has with the burdens of life that weighs on the dispossessed and not knowing when the salvation will appear."

The important thing here is 'hope'. Yes, teenagers think their lives are shit, but they *hope* that they won't be, and it's that hope that makes their lives shit. Your job is to either make them abandon all hope, or, more helpfully, let them see a light at the end of their despair-ridden tunnel.

* Not literally

Let's start by establishing what they actually worry about:

I'm different to other people
I'm not different enough
School will never end
What the hell do I do when it does?
I'm too fat
I'm too thin
Noah/Chloe doesn't fancy me
Noah/Chloe is being too clingy
My mum's, like, so unfair
My dad's, like, so unfair
Life's, like, so unfair
I'm being groomed on Twitter
No one on Twitter fancies me
Mum won't let me wear make up
Why do people think I'm a tart?
My friends are pressuring me to take drugs
My friends won't give me any of their drugs
I'm going to flunk my exams
If I pass too many I'll be called a swot
Why am I bleeding? Am I dying?
Why am I late? Am I pregnant?
My breast buds make me feel self-conscious
I'm so overweight, I'm not sure they even *are* breast buds
I think I might be gay
I think I might be rejected by my LGBT friends if they suss out I'm straight

So many concerns for one so young. But each of these worries can be dealt with by an empathetic and wise father. But if you can't find one of those, it'll come down to you*.

* You can pass on the ones about periods, breast buds and make up to your wife, unless it's your son who's concerned about them

How to allay their fears:
Step 1: Dismiss their worries
Say they are fretting needlessly, that their concerns are baseless and that there is every possibility it won't be as bad as they think.

Step 2: Your childhood
Assure them that you went through something very similar, that it was fine 'in the end' and that you soon got over it. Even if you never did

Step 3: Blame their bodies
The stress they are feeling isn't because of an *actual* thing, it's an *imagined* thing caused by the things going on inside their heads. Once they get to twenty, things will get easier. Saying 'things' exempts you from any complicated scientific explanations.

Step 4: Distract them
I know you're worried about X, but actually, it might be better to worry about Y.

Step 5: Convince them it's character building
We are the sum of all our experiences, so though this might seem bad (and indeed *be* bad) one day you'll realise it has made you a stronger person. And the next six years will whiz past, hopefully.

Step 6: Get a grip!
Yes, it's not fair, but life's not fair. So pull yourself together, stop the hand wringing and go get your dad a beer.

Step 7: Threaten them
If you don't stop going on about this, you'll be sent to your room. How many times do I have to tell you that worrying won't make it go away.

Step 8: Say: 'Go speak with your mother'
After all, you can only do so much and they've bleated on enough.

There is another way to cheer them up, however: the dad joke.

Dad jokes

When you become a father, you don't lose your sense of humour, it just changes. Gone are the witty throwaway lines that always had your friends in hysterics, gone is the political satire, the carefree gags you invented on the spot.

Having kids causes a metaphysical change in the brain that renders all attempts at laugh-inducement futile.

In the place of your formerly comedic genius is the Dad Joke.

They have three characteristics:
1. They are not remotely funny
2. They are extremely funny to the dad concerned.
3. They will embarrass any family members present

When telling a dad joke, it's vital to laugh very loudly and uncontrollably at the end so that everyone knows that you have just delivered the punchline. Failure to do this will result in perplexed, slightly pitying faces, a period of silence followed by a polite 'pardon?'.

So, let's consider some ground rules…

1. The double entendre
Whenever anyone says something that could have another, slightly rude, meaning, you are duty bound to point it out.

Examples might include:
d) Have you given her one?
e) Can you get it in?
f) Do you want some?
g) Is it a tight fit?
h) Would you like a large portion?

i) Is there room on top?
j) Did it take long to erect it?
k) Is it big enough?
l) Can anyone fill me in?
m) Does your bush need a trim?
n) Are you coming?

If any of these are ever uttered, you need to immediately add something like '...as the actress said to the bishop!' or 'oo-er missus' or 'ooh, sounds a bit rude, know what I mean, eh?'

Then, you should burst into laughter, and, if those around still haven't got your priceless joke, jab them in the stomach and continue giggling.

When your teenage kids stare contemptuously at you, and say 'Daaad!' through clenched teeth, it means you're on course.

2. References to alcohol (mainly beer)

If it's after 10.30am, then this means you can start implying that you'd like a drink: 'I see the sun's over the yard arm', 'ah, beer o'clock', 'fancy a quickie? Eh? Eh?'.

Then, when you take your first slurp, sigh loudly in satisfaction and call it 'Daddy's special medicine'.

The other thing is to suggest that every night out you've ever had became a full-on booze fest of epic proportions. Teenagers and non-dads have done this for centuries, but the difference for the dad is that the story is patently not true.

Even if your night out was to go to Posey's parent teacher evening, when telling your mates, you will insist that: a) You can't remember getting home, b) the barmaid was chatting you up, c) your mate did something hilarious when he was drunk and d) the amount of alcohol you consumed would kill the average gorilla.

3. Clothing

There are ten-year-old kids in sweatshops on the Indian sub continent who spend seventy hours a week producing t-shirts for dads.

It's a specialist market because no one else would ever be seen dead in them.

Possible designs include:
1. I'm with stupid
2. Homer Simpson clutching a beer
3. 'World's greatest dad'
4. Will work for beer
5. Sex instructor –first lesson free
6. I'm only here for the beer
7. You don't have to be mad to work here… but it helps!
8. BBQ king
9. F.B.I. Female body inspector

Dad jokes for different ages

Every comedian adjusts his routine slightly to suit the audience, and you'll need to do the same as your children grow up. Although your lack of humour will be what mathematicians call a 'constant' throughout their childhoods, the reactions will vary considerably.

Here's a very basic guide:

0-4 months

You will try a multitude of increasingly desperate things to make them laugh, and get precisely no response. They will stare blankly in random directions as if you weren't there and maybe emit a burp or even vomit if they have just been drinking. You will worry that they are brain damaged

5-months-5 years

This bit's easy. Everything you do is funny. Your mere presence is enough to make them laugh uncontrollably. Silly walks, pulling your face into weird expressions and peek-a-boo is proof they have literally the funniest daddy who has ever walked the Earth. There is no need for *actual* jokes as they will crack up if you read out the Yellow Pages in a funny voice.

6-11 years

These are your prime years for jokes. It's still too soon for any involving nuns in a bath, but any one liner with a lame pun is comedy gold. And, unlike anyone else with an IQ over forty, they still love it when Daddy mucks around and acts the fool.

12-15 years

Trickier. They have now realised that not every one of your jokes is necessarily funny. In fact, probably none of them are. They will laugh if a joke is 'a bit rude', but hold fire on the nun joke for a while yet. Even the hilarity of pretending to walk downstairs behind the kitchen counter may wear thin.

16-19 years

You will try a multitude of increasingly desperate things to make them laugh, and get precisely no response. They will stare blankly in random directions as if you weren't there and maybe emit a burp or even vomit if they have just been drinking. You will worry that they are brain damaged.

Are all other dads better than you?

A six-year-old who lives with her seven siblings and chain-smoking parents in a beat up caravan parked next to Cirencester Ring Road has no idea that her life is shit.

Why would she? Like a goldfish in a bowl, she has known no different.

But while the gullible old fish is unlikely to ever start questioning why he swims around in his own excrement all day, the child will at some point realise that some of her friends live in nicer houses. And before long, her innocent mind will start to ponder why this might be. Is it luck? Is it because her own parents *like* living like gypsies? Or could it be that these other children have a better daddy? A daddy who is more successful.

This might be an extreme example, and no one likes being compared to a disgruntled guppy, but your teenager will become aware of the concept of class* and that, though she still loves you lots and lots, it might be worth looking at other dad options.

Do your child's friends have more impressive fathers?
If you're not sure, then they probably do, but let's not jump to conclusions until you've completed this morale-draining quiz...

1. Do you in fact live in a caravan on Cirencester Ring Road?
No! Well, actually yes, but only until we're moved on - 5 points
No, but maybe our gardener does +5 points

2. Has your teenager introduced you to any of his or her friends?
Yes, er, when she was in kindy she did -10 points
She has friends? - 5 points
Not since the school disco 'incident' -12 points

3. Do they ask you to drop them off round the corner from the school rather than at the gates?
Yes, but he says it's safer that way -3 points
Only if I'm driving my ice cream van -4 points
Not since I got the Ferrari +20 points

* And your lack of it

4. Gavin and Stacey are
Comically exaggerated pikeys +4 points
Too posh and snobby for their own good -16 points

5. Which of the following do you own?
Race horse +30 points
Yacht +22 points
Apron with boobies on   -9 points
Mullet -3 points
'Honk if you're horny' bumper sticker -14 points
Wall mounted badger head -18 points
Ecstasy making apparatus -27 points

6. What in the house has to be hidden before your teenager brings friends round?
Faberge eggs and Rembrandt originals + 23 points
Keys to the Aston Martin + 19 points
Your Gollum tattoo -28 points

7. Your children call you:
a) Pater + 8 points
b) Dad + 1 point
c) During visiting hours -29 points

Over 40 points
You can breathe easy – other fathers *aren't* better than you, possibly because you're European royalty

Between -19 and 39 points
Your teenager isn't totally embarrassed by you as long as you don't actually speak to their friends. Most of her friends have a dad who is better looking, more respectable and doesn't think breaking wind is amusing.

Under -20

There are breeds of weasel that make better dads than you. Your teenagers will beg their friends' parents to adopt them.

So, yes, other parents are less embarrassing then you are. They drive cars that aren't customized, don't stick an 'o' on the end of every name and haven't hung a signed poster of David Essex in the living room.

But, wait a sec – all of this pre supposes that your teenager being ashamed of you is a *bad* thing. If you think this, you haven't been paying attention.

Exactly when did your kids start judging you so harshly?* And when did you start caring?

The point is that one of the few joys of having teenage kids is making them so hideously embarrassed they wish they'd never been born. If you went through it with your parents, why shouldn't they? It's part of growing up, and will better equip them for all the shame and humiliation they'll experience in later life.

Fun ways to embarrass your teenager

All of these should be done in front of one or more of their friends...

Talk about your sex life
Ask then to buy their mum some tampons
Put their childhood teddy in their bed when they bring their mates round
Talk in gangsta speak
Ask them if their 'little rash' has cleared up
Frame their acne-plagued school photos

* When that's the job of your assigned care in the community worker and the presiding magistrate

Beep the horn whenever you pick them up
Put Tweenies yogurt in their lunchbox
Disco dance in the kitchen
Ask them why their taste in music is so diabolical
Tell them it's time for the 'birds and bees' conversation
Wear Speedos
To a girl: ask if it's time for their first bra
To a boy: ask if they've had a wet dream
Lick your finger and wipe their cheek clean with it
Talk in a Yoda voice: 'Good to see you, it is'
Walk round the house naked
Demand to know if it was them who blocked the toilet
When you drop them off for a sleepover, tell them loudly: 'I packed some extra jimmies, just in case'
Ask their friends if they'll submit to a random drugs test
Talk about your time as a Scientologist
Say: 'Is it tickle time? I think it is!'
Show the first boyfriend/girlfriend your child's breastfeeding photos
Reassure them that masturbation is perfectly normal at their age and they shouldn't feel awkward that you found the evidence.
Accuse him of stealing your Viagra

These should have the desired effect, though one issue might be that you rarely see their friends as all their interactions are now online. Fortunately, this needn't stop you…

Online humiliations

If a guy is suggestively posting on your daughter's timeline, change you profile pic to one of you holding a shotgun
Tag them literally everywhere you go with them
Befriend all their friends

If one of their mates suggests going out, post: 'Sorry, Becky, but Ellie is still grounded'

Help them find love by finding one of their attractive friends and posting: 'You seem like a nice boy/girl – have you thought about asking my son/daughter out?'

Tweet regular updates on your daughter's menstrual cycle

Post up naked baby pictures making reference to the size of genitalia not being much different these days.

Write them a reference on Linked In that mentions their 10m breaststroke badge and Ballet Star Performer 2003 Award.

Tweet news of her first period

Grooming

These days, internet grooming is a very real problem. Children befriend someone masquerading as a child of their age and can find themselves lured into dangerous situations after weeks of seemingly innocent conversations. As a father, you need to be aware of this threat. The best advice is to persuade your kids not to groom anyone. Tell them it's rude.

Are your kids taking drugs?

There are probably three main dangers facing your kids that will terrify you beyond all others: that he/she might: a) Be involved in a car accident, b) Take drugs or c) Join UKIP.

And you're right to be concerned*. But, if it's any consolation, there are hundreds of other ways your child could come to grief, so there's no point in dwelling solely on these three.

For now, though, let's take drugs. Not literally take them ourselves (plenty of time for that later when you've finished this chapter), but take a look at the issues.

* Especially if they're toking on a spliff while driving to hear Nigel Farage speak.

Children can become exposed to illegal substances as early as nine or ten*, usually by their friends or their friends' older brothers or sisters. Your first step, therefore is to ban your child from having any friends who have older brothers and sisters.

Then you need to sit them down and calmly talk about peer pressure and how they will respond when offered their first joint.

Read this case history to see how one father (we'll call him Bob**) handled this potentially difficult conversation:

Bob: Ah, Tommy, can I borrow you for a couple of minutes. We need to have a chat.

Tommy: Ah Dad this isn't about sex is it?

Bob: Er, no your, um, mother will talk you through that at some point.

Tommy: Well what then? I'm late for my tennis lesson

Bob: This won't take too long. Son, now you're a teenager, you're going to come until contact with some pretty shading characters, and...

Tommy: You mean like Uncle Niall

Bob: Yes, er, I mean no. I mean, er, people who may offer you illegal substances

Tommy: You *do* mean Uncle Niall.

Bob: No, listen, this is important. Soon, one of your friends may suggest that taking drugs is cool.

Tommy: Well, isn't it?

Bob: No! No, it's not cool, it's very *uncool*, very wicked.

Tommy: Dad, wicked means good remember

Bob: Stop, interrupting son. The thing about drugs is that they may seem harmless enough, but they are very addictive and once you start, it's very hard to stop.

* Earlier if they have the keys to your bedside table
** Because that's his name

Tommy: Did *you* ever take them, Dad?

Bob: Did I, er, well… well, that's not what I'm talking about now. These days, marijuana can ruin your life, and…

Tommy: Did it ruin *your* life?

Bob: Ha, no, it… Er, I mean, yes, it did, and…

Tommy: But your life is great. You've got a great job, drive an Audi, and…

Bob: Tommy, you're missing the point. Once you start taking drug…

Tommy: Did you manage to stop taking them?

Bob: Of course I did. But that was a long time ago.

Tommy: So they *didn't* ruin your life, and you *did* manage to stop taking them. Did Mum take them too?

Bob: Oh yes, in fact, er, I mean, listen, son, that's not the issue. If you want to do well at school, then…

Tommy: But you got straight As and a masters degree. And so did Mum.

Bob: Yes, but drugs are expensive these days and money doesn't grow on…

Tommy: Uncle Niall sells a gram for only £50

Bob: £50? Wow, that is very, er, hang on. I forbid you to take it because it will turn you into a feckless dopehead and you'll never get a job. Do you hear me?

Tommy: So how come you keep joints in your bait tin?

Bob: In my…? How dare you look in there. That is private. If a man can't have some privacy, then it's… well, it's… Oh forgot it, here's £50 or next time you see Niall. Tell him I don't want any rubbish, mind.

Tommy: Fine. Can I go to tennis now?

Clues they may already be taking drugs

Usually it's the parents who are last to know that their children have turned into psychotic smackheads robbing gastro pubs or turning tricks to feed their habit. And it can be embarrassing when you only find out when their story forms the basis of a Panorama Special.

Look for signs like these:

Jamaica flag in bedroom, but he has no idea who Usain Bolt is
Her two nostrils have now become one
When he takes a bank note out of his wallet, it seems to curl up
Refuses cold turkey
Laughs uncontrollably at your lame jokes
Is convinced she's a reincarnation of Amy Winehouse
Wants to enter the Tour de France but has never cycled
Says 'yer, man' in nearly every sentence
Claims that the white powder wrapped in a condom they were swallowing before the flight was just a vitamin supplement.
Doritos missing from cupboard
Claims the used syringes in her bin are because she thinks she might be diabetic
Affects a West Indian patois at all social gatherings
Insists that pock marks on arms are the result of acupuncture
Sporting heroes are Ben Johnson and Lance Armstrong
They suggest moving to either Wrexham or Columbia

OK, so we've established beyond all* reasonable doubt that they are taking something, and it's not purely medicinal. Clearly their mother has failed them. But before we overreact, let's consider a couple of points: a) There's a chance they aren't heroin junkies or sprinkling crystal meths on their breakfast cereal, and b) They're probably too spaced out to do real damage to your property or any passing law enforcement officers.

* Some

10

The Birds and the Bees

*"Birds do it, bees do it, even educated fleas do it.
Let's do it, let's fall in love"*
*~ **Cole Porter***

"What a kid I got, I told him about the birds and the bees, and he told me about the butcher and my wife"
*~ **Rodney Dangerfield***

If you were given this book because you're about to enter fatherhood*, then it must seem very odd for us to be talking about sex. You're going to have a little baby who will always be wide eyed and innocent of the world's more tawdry pursuits**.

Equally, it's very odd staring at a spotty, six foot four inch 18-year-old prop forward and remembering a time when they were innocent of anything.

Somewhere in between these two, lies the age when children first start to be aware of sex.

Usually, before the onset of puberty, it comes from playground banter, an older friend, one of mum's magazines, a biology lesson or a Catholic priest. And it can be confusing and frightening for them.

---

* Or stole a copy. Wait, can you steal an ebook?
** I mean sex, not working for a major bank

And for some reason, throughout human history, it's the father who is expected to have the little chat known for some reason as 'the birds and the bees'.

If it was called the 'dogs and the cats' then at least the child might have actually witnessed the act themselves and therefore have a basic grounding. But no, few adults let alone children, have actually witnessed birds or bees copulating and there's a danger that the very literal child will surmise that he has to deposit pollen somewhere or get his wife to lay an egg. So there's probably no need for you to use it as a metaphor*.

Anyway, no point getting distracted by the title of the talk you're about to deliver, we need to think about the contents.

Firstly, what exactly are you going to tell them? Everything? The basics? And what do they already know? You don't want your little chat to turn out like this:

Father: You're at the age now when I need to talk to you about sex
Child: Sure, dad, what do you want to know?

So before you go ahead, have a checklist of facts they need to know, and leave the rest for their sex education lesson at school. Failing that, stick on Monty Python's Meaning of Life.

What exactly do you need to include?

Tell them: That when a man and a woman love each other something very special can happen

Don't tell them: The woman often requires alcohol before she will consent

Tell them: A man and a woman get married before they do this special thing

Don't tell them: Sometimes the man will attempt it with someone else on his stag night

* Not even the fact that, as with bees, a sticky substance is produced

Tell them: Men and women are built a little differently
Don't tell them: And I can see from the way you're built, son, that you won't be embarrassed in the showers.

Tell them: A man puts his penis into the lady's vagina
Don't tell them: Foreplay is so called because it must last no longer than four minutes

Tell them: A little seed comes out of daddy and swims into Mummy
Don't tell them: Mostly, Mummy kills them with spermicide

Tell them: Every month, Mummy produces an egg
Don't tell them: The eggs you eat for breakfast are chicken's periods

Tell them: Lots of Daddy's little seeds try to get to Mummy's egg
Don't tell them: Actually, since Mummy forced you to have the snip, millions of them die every day and their corpses rot in your testicles

Tell them: Only one of them can make it inside to fertilise the egg
Don't tell them: So for you to be born, you effectively killed off 200 million of your brothers and sisters

Tell them: If Mummy and Daddy don't want to have a baby, then Daddy can wear something called a condom
Don't tell them: Mummy prefers ultra thin, non-lubricated

Tell them: When the egg has been fertilized, it lodges in the lining of the uterus.
Don't tell them: ...and it's a minor miracle that Daddy's penis didn't dislodge it, given its impressive size

Tell them: The little foetus grows for nine months before it is ready to be born

Don't tell them: Mummy's boobs get bigger and she craves sex even more for the first few months

For a boy:
Tell them: Soon you'll have something called a wet dream
Don't tell them: But there are more fun ways of getting the same result

For a girl:
Tell them: Your menstrual cycle means you will bleed for a day or two every month
Don't tell them: And thank Christ Mummy is nearing an age when she won't be grumpy to Daddy during that time

How to handle awkward questions

Even though you've taken the time to explain to them about the mechanics of sexual intercourse, some children still aren't satisfied. So your awkward little talk may enter a Q&A session as they seek more information than is actually good for them. If this happens, then the best thing to do is fob them off with an answer that sounds real enough and will do until their mates tell them the truth. Here's how to do it:

Question: Why are some condoms ribbed?
Answer: It makes them stronger, and helps them grip on a bit more

Q: Why do adults use toys? Aren't you a bit old?
A: You never heard of Meccano? Or Rubik's Cube? Of course adults like toys

Q: How come I was born only seven months before you got married?
A: Well, you know when I'm mad at you and call you a little bastard? Well…

Q: What's a G spot? Do I have one?
A: You mean G-Force. It was a film about super hero guinea pigs.

Q: Does Mummy scream because it hurts?
A: No, were watching a scary movie. Well, a movie that was scary for thirty seconds.

Q: Doesn't Mummy get squashed as you're so fat?
That's why she's nice and slim.

Q: Why are my older brother's sheets sometimes all crinkly?
Some new washing powder your mum's bought. Yours will probably be the same quite soon.

Q: Am I a twin because you had sex twice?
Yes

Q: Did I inherit my small willy from you?
No, the size is passed through the genes from the mother's side. But best don't mention it to Gramps.

10 reasons your son really doesn't want to become a father

If you have a teenage boy, then you also have a sex-crazed impregnating machine, casually spraying his juices over the teenage girls in your neighbourhood and surrounding suburbs*.

And, as we all know, when a young lad is in mid-spray he's not necessarily assessing the impact fatherhood would have on his ability to charm the undies off future conquests.

* Especially if you successfully stopped him being a nerd

And it's your job to put the fear of God into him about the possible consequences of his actions. Especially if her father has links to the Manchester underworld.

As he probably won't listen to reason, just give him these facts to digest…

1. Playing Black Ops 2 isn't as easy while rocking a baby to sleep.
2. There are no crèches in Ibiza
3. He could technically be a granddad by the time he's 28.
4. It's the *mother* not the father who gets drugs during childbirth.
5. He'll have to take down the Megan Fox posters from his bedroom (now also known as the nursery).
6. His Gap Year will become a year shopping at Baby Gap.
7. Teachers frown on bringing a baby to show and tell.
8. Hot babes don't want another babe on the date.
9. You don't want a mother-in-law turning up to your prom.
10. It's awkward asking the mother of your unborn child to remind you of her name.

Is your child gay?

A Child's sexual feelings can start with a crush on a pop singer or Twilight star, and are harmless enough (assuming the pop singer isn't Pete Townsend).

But they will also know to which gender they are attracted, so you need to manage your expectations about whether one day you'll have a houseful of grandchildren, or be decorating a float on a Pride march.

Clues your daughter may be gay
Chaz Bono poster above bed
Actively looking for a Barbie boiler suit on ebay
Ken fitted for padded bra

Starts planning boob reduction surgery while still in primary school
Uses mascara to enhance moustache
You're given an invite to My Little Pony's civil union.
Toilet seats in dolls house permanently down
Refuses to eat hotdogs, cucumbers or bananas

Clues your son may be gay
Toy soldiers forced to drop 'Don't ask, don't tell' policy.
Action Man wears make up and participates in revival of Cabaret
Engages in Twitter speculation as to his favourite member of One Direction
Insists on dressing as flamboyant Cherokee brave during Cowboys and Indians
Fakes note from you to avoid PE, but still showers
Considers Roger Moore to be the best James Bond
Overly proud of animal print shoes

Their first boyfriend or girlfriend

This section isn't about the boy or girl they slyly kiss in the playground in Year 1. They don't count as a) there was no long term commitment, and b) they only did it to get a Milky Bar.

No, the first proper relationship won't happen until at least fifteen, and probably older. The first thing you'll notice is much blushing going on when this person's name is mentioned. This means that either they have feeling for them or they have early onset rosacea.

As their father, you're first act is to say in front of the rest of the family and/or their closest friends in what you think is a hilarious voice: 'Has my little boy got a girlfriend?! Has he? I think he has! Ooh – what's her name then? Is it Emily? It is isn't it?'

This will immediately put them at ease and show that you empathise with any embarrassment they may be feeling.

If they are indeed fifteen, then they will have been dumped by the end of the week and will start regretting that self-administered tattoo of her name they scratched into their arm.

If they are sixteen, it may last another week before one of them snogs someone else in the chemistry lab.

By seventeen, it starts getting 'serious'*.

That's when, as their father, you need to be involved. Among the questions you need to ask yourself are:

Is he good enough for my daughter?

Does he have any visible tattoos?
Yes
No

Are his family members of the traveling community?
Yes
No

Is he clinically obese?
Yes
No

Does he still have all his own teeth?
Yes
No

Does he have a condom attached to his keyring?
Yes
No

Is he a member of an illegal gang of bikers?
Yes
No

* Involving sex, that is, not 'solemn and thoughtful in nature'

Did he make it past Year 9 at school?
Yes
No

Has he ever been a member of Status Quo?
Yes
No

Has he been married more than three times before?
Yes
No

Where does he want to take your daughter on their first date
To see a film
Past third base

Results

Number of questions answered 'yes'

0-1

He's far too good for her and can clearly do much better. Tell her to enjoy it while it lasts.

2-3

He sounds like he's better bred than your daughter, and she might realise what a crap father you've been all these years.

4-6

He's perfect! Tell her she needs to marry him straight away and get pregnant so she holds on to him.

7-9

He's not quite the son-in-law you hoped for, but at least he's out of prison now.

All 10

She'd be better of marrying Shane Warne.

Is she good enough for your son?

Do you recognize her from that 'gentleman's club' you go to?
Yes: - 3 points
No: + 2

Has she had more than one kid from different prisoners?
Yes: - 7
No: + 1

Has she ever been rejected by Big Brother for being too lewd?
Yes: - 2
No: + 1

Is she more than seven inches taller than your son?
Yes: - 10
No: + 4

Her school report concluded she'd make an excellent
Homemaker: + 3
Lingerie model: -3

Is her father the leader of an African nation?
Yes: -1
No: + 1

Has she taken or is she taking any subjects that end on 'ology'?
Yes: - 7
No: + 4

Is she related to Kerry Katona?
Yes: -16
No: + 2

Has she ever been in a hotel room with seven or more Premier League players?
Yes: -3
No: + 1

Has she ever been sentenced to 20 years in a Singapore jail for smuggling drugs in her vagina?
Yes: - 2
No: + 0.5

+ 15 OR MORE
Yes, I'm afraid she is Pippa Middleton and therefore far too good for your spotty-arsed son

BETWEEN 10 AND 14
On the plus side she'll teach him some manners, on the down side she may try to teach you some too

BETWEEN 2 AND 9
She's the one! Tell him that this girl is even hotter than his mother was at that age, and that he'd better make a move or you'll get in before him

BETWEEN -3 AND 1
She makes Kat Slater look like Kate Middleton, but keep hold of her number in case all other options run out

LESS THAN -3

Has several species of fungus growing on her, which explains the smell of mildew. At least her hydroponics apparatus means the house is nice and warm at night.

Is YOUR daughter a hooker?

There are millions of prostitutes out there, and all of them had a father at some point. One just like you. Or maybe a bit more creepy than you. The point is, very few of them will be aware that the 'beauty salon' they think she works at to supplement her college fees offers a more personal service than the one your wife goes to.

Unless your wife is *also* on the game, that is. But let's leave that probability to one side for now.

It's your daughter we're worried about. Has she had a little *too* much sex education and, unlike her food science, is she now seeing a lucrative vocational side to it? If, after reading this, you're suddenly terrified that, since she moved out, she might be ungainfully employed to pay her university fees, you might be right.

But before you make too many unfounded accusations in front of her new boyfriend* , take this handy quiz...

1. When you call her at work to see how she is, she answers:
a) A Hello, Sarah speaking
b) C Look, Stavros, how many times do I have to tell you that if you want extras, you'll have to speak to my pimp.

2. You ask her what she'd like for Christmas she replies
a) Book token or some smellies.
b) Crotchless knickers and a black leather cat o' nine tales

3. You phone her while she's in the car, she says:
a) Sorry Dad, I'll call you when I get home
b) Sorry, Dad, but I can't speak with my mouth full

4. Her new bedroom suite includes a

a) Walk in wardrobe and dressing table
b) Turnstile

5. She rents a nice little flat:
a) By the park
b) By the hour

* Or client

Mostly As: Relax! She's not a sex worker. Not yet, anyway. Those notches in the bedpost must be woodworm.

Mostly Bs: Relax! She's a sex worker. So what? There are worse ways to earn a living, aren't there? No? Well, stop relaxing and start driving to all the brothels in your area, demand to see every girl they have on their books and take the girls into a private room so you can thoroughly pump them for information as regards your daughter.

11
Adult children

"I was thrown out of college for cheating on the metaphysics exam: I looked into the soul of another boy."
~ Woody Allen

All who curse their father or mother must be put to death. They are guilty of a capital offense.
~ Leviticus 20:9

In traditional cultures, elders are venerated and respected givers of wisdom. Their adult children look to them for advice on how to appease the Gods, grow strong harvests, hunt monkeys and master Instagram.

At feasts, they sit at the high table and make pronouncements on issues like which village to attack next, how many wives they're taking that week or which goat is to be sacrificially slaughtered to ensure an end to the rainy season.

No one would dare question them or challenge their authority in case they made them very cross.

If only such primitive values were true elsewhere. If only our ungrateful kin would throw themselves at out feet self-flagellating and declaring themselves unworthy of even being in our company. And if only they would retain that misty-eyed wonder that a child has for its dad, the person it looks up to and idolises more than any other.

As soon as our children are old enough to leave home we only see them when they run out of cash, have been kicked out of their share house or want to borrow the car.

Our opinions are dismissed as the feeble ramblings of a elderly dinosaur long past its extinct-by date, and any advice we proffer is patronizingly dismissed as lunacy*.

What's hard to take as a father is that the little boy or girl you raised no longer *needs* you. They have somehow gone from dependants to independents, and are probably taller than you as well.

But all this doesn't mean that you aren't involved in their lives, nor, sadly, that there are fewer areas of stress involved.

Kids will try to kid you that they may be *your* kids, but they're not *kids* anymore. But are they? When does a child officially become an adult?

When they're old enough to drive to a new house? Or be sent to an adult prison?

Are they adults when they enter college?

This quiz may help:

1. Is your child over the age of eighteen?
a) Yes
b) No

Mostly As

Congratulations! Your child is an adult, and as such they are now responsible for their own actions. If you were a species other than human, you would never have to see them again.

Mostly Bs

Hmm, sorry, but our calculations show that your child is not an adult. There is, however, evidence that he or she may become one in the coming years.

* And, yes, sometimes it is. But that's not the point.

You see, it's not up to them to decide when they're ready to be adults (or indeed you), it's decided by society. If you're eighteen, then suck it up – you're not a juvenile anymore, and won't be able to rely on Daddy's not so deep pockets.

And don't think about kicking up a fuss or you'll be sent to you room. Or rather, you can send yourself to your room because we're not going to do it for you.

So, you have an adult living with you. But where to now? College? Well, hopefully, but before you get too excited, let's address whether further education might take them a little outside their comfort zone*.

Is your child too stupid for college?

1. At school they excel at:
a) Maths, science and French literature
b) Sexting
2. They were voted most likely to:
a) Succeed
b) Be sentenced to death by firing squad

3. In their GCSEs they got straight…
a) …As
b) …up, the worst results in the school's history

4. Their priority after leaving school is to pick…
a) The right uni degree to suit their skills
b) Fruit

5. Their most productive extra curricular activity was
c) Debating
d) Masturbating

* ie Are they brain dead?

6. Their head teacher said he was:
a) Sorry to see them leave
b) Sorry they were ever born

7. He also said he'd like them to return:
a) To give a talk to the younger children
b) The sports equipment they swiped

8. A prestigious university has already:
a) Offered them a scholarship
b) Taken out a restraining order

9. They've got 90%:
a) In their Chemistry exam
b) Fewer brain cells than Gazza

10. They'll miss their school friends, but…
a) …they will keep in touch through Facebook and reunions
b) …with good behaviour, they should be free to see them again in a couple of years

Mostly As

Good news – they take after you and are easily clever enough for college! Bad news – they're also insufferable swots and will be bullied accordingly.

Mostly Bs

Good news – no college fees to pay! Bad news – they take after their mother and have the intellectual capacity of a jellyfish.

Sadly not everyone can go to college. Well, it's not *really* sad as it'd be a waste of resources if you spent four years in tutorials and lectures training to be cage dancers at Stringfellow's. But just because your kid doesn't get a place it doesn't mean you've failed. There's every chance someone else failed instead.

Just remember that list of celebrities in Chapter Seven who flunked out of school. But don't turn to it now or you may also find the advice on making your kids smarter that you clearly didn't take.

Another issue with children who don't go to university is that they have a nasty habit of not leaving home because they don't earn enough. They do somehow earn enough to go drinking every night, smoke twenty a day, enjoy weekends in St Tropez and buy designer trainers, but after paying for all of those, there's nothing left over for luxuries like rent.

How to get them to move out
Take their bedroom door off its hinges
Attach a padlock to the fridge
Announce that Auntie Hilda will be sharing their room from now on
Set up CCTV in the bathroom
Unsubscribe from Sky Sports
Invite a priest round to exorcise the poltergeist under their bed
Don't let them leave the table until they've eaten their greens
Play your Emerson, Lake and Palmer CDs at full volume for several hours each day
Change the broadband password five times a week
Teach the mynah bird to say 'You still here, Timmy?'
Put a red sock in with all their white washing
Insist they say Grace before every meal
Include 'yo diggity' in every sentence
Electrify the handrail above the bath

OK, job done. They're either at university (probably not learning much amid the drinking) or at work (probably not earning much amid the drinking). Either way, they're gone. The room where you once read them stories, tucked them into bed and watched them gently sleep is now empty save for a few Eminem posters, their failed woodwork projects and a faint smell of cannabis resin.

You have an empty nest and, as luck would have it, someone has invented a syndrome of that very name. You see, strange as this may seem, when your brood leaves, so does a little bit of you.

Actually, that's bollocks. Forget I ever wrote it. I'd delete it right now if only my delete button worked.

When you get the house to yourself, life begins again. Though do look out for subtle signs that your missus might be suffering. Things like:

Adopts a Somalian refugee
Starts engaging in conversation with pigeons
Buys life size dolls and names them after your children
Starts reading you bedtime stories
Still sets five places at the dinner table
Tells you that you can't get down until you've finished your parnsips
Buys the dog a waistcoat
Starts engaging in conversation with *other* bird species
Feigns a phantom pregnancy

Chances are she'll get over it after a few months of crushing emptiness and a gnawing sense of uselessness. As you'll be familiar with the latter you can reassure her that there is still a purpose in her life, and it's not as though the kids have all upped sticks and moved to Eastern Europe*.

And your role as a father might not be a full-time job any more** but that doesn't mean it stops all together. For a start, there are lots of ways adult children can be lead astray. You need to remain vigilant.

*Unless they are in fact leaving to live in Eastern Europe
** Who are we kidding? At best you were a casual shift worker

Paul Merrill

Is your daughter a terrorist?

Fact: more suicide bombers are female than male. Fact: crazed and dangerous women have fooled men for centuries with their feminine charms and no-strings-attached sex.

It goes to follow, therefore, that all women have the potential to become deranged extremists intent on the overthrow of decadent western society.

Even the sweet-natured daughter who loved her rabbits could have grown up into a fully-fledge bunny boiler.

Concerned? Yes, well, you might have good reason. But before you tip off the Scotland Yard, take this little quiz just to be sure...

1. Her last holiday was to:
A Club 18-30 coach tour
B Former Taliban training camp outside Kabul

2. When she was growing up, she'd beg to go:
A: Maccas
B: Mecca

3. The photo by her bedside is:
A: Her pet cat, Fluffy
B: Ayman al-Zawahiri

4. At the garden centre last week, she bought
A: A rose cutting and tub of geraniums
B: Three tons of fertiliser

5. To discipline her own children, she:
A: Sends them to bed early
B: Uses handcuffs, sleep-deprivation, water boarding and Alsatians

6. At her comprehensive, she was voted
A: The girl most likely to succeed
B: The girl most likely to explode

6. For her own personal protection, she always carries:
A: A whistle and can of mace
B: AK-47 and Semtex

7. One day she hopes to meet
A: Justin Bieber
B: 72 Virgins

Mostly As: There's a chance she's not a terrorist, but have her phone tapped just in case

Mostly Bs: She's the commander of an Al Qaeda terror cell plotting an imminent suicide mission. Tell her she's not too old to be put over your knee.

Grandchildren

Jeez, we're at grandchildren already? A few pages back we were happily discussing ways to stop them crying and nappy changing! Well, guess what, those same skills are going to be called on again, only this time it's not even your kid.

There is a lot you need to know about becoming a grandparent, but there isn't the space here. As luck would have it, my next book, *Muddle Your Way Through Being a Grandparent* will contain everything you need to know plus a whole lot that isn't strictly necessary, but I had promised a certain wordcount so had to pad it out a bit towards the end. The same isn't true of this book which is definitely, definitely, definitely, definitely, definitely, definitely, definitely long enough.

In fact if you were a decent father you'd buy the grandparenting book for *your* parents as soon as you become a dad thereby killing two birds with one book: 1.) They'll thank you for such a thoughtful present, and 2) they'll learn to be less worse grandparents. So everyone's a winner*

Are your children racist

When you're gently rocking a baby to sleep, it's hard to imagine that one day it might turn into an evil fascist and join a white supremacist movement in Bradford dedicated to the establishment of an Aryan super race the likes of which can only be found in Hitler's wet dreams and the villages in Midsomer Murders.

Yes, that cute, gurgling little thing could, even now, be harbouring dreams of ethnically cleansing Toytown.

This quiz will hopefully put your mind at rest.

1. What do they consider the world's deadliest race?
The Dakar (-5 points)
The Arabs (+ 5 pints)

2. Which of these do they own?
White robe and hood (+ 15 points)
Signed copy of Desmond Tutu's autobiography (-5 points)
Union Jack tattoo (+ 3 points)
Wok (-8 points)
A concubine (+ 12 point)
Bob Marley record (-2 points)

3. Their favourite charity is:
Oxfam (-4 points)
Red Cross (+1 point)
Let's Keep Basingstoke White (+ 3 points)
Mel Gibson (+ 17 points)

* Including my creditors

You've caught them masturbating to:
Naomi Campbell (-4 points)
The slave auction in Roots (+ 10 points)

When buying dips, you ask them if they like hummus, do they say
Thank you, perfect with the tabouli (-8 points)
No, ketchup was good enough for my father and it's good enough for me (+ 2 points)

Which of the following tapes did they send in to You've Been Framed?
A Kid falling over (0 point)
A black kid falling over (+ 3 points)
The Rodney King tape (+ 9 points)

At night they fall asleep cuddling:
A sheet (0 points)
A sheet with two eye holes cut out (+ 4 points)
Golliwog with string round its neck (+ 12 points)
Their copy of Mein Kampf (+ 15 points)

When they get a little cross, do they:
Shout and scream (0 points)
Set fire to it and put it on the black neighbour's lawn (+ 30 points)

-25 to -1 points: Relax, they are not racist.
0 to 25 points: They're not so much racist as stupid. A clip round the ear and copy of Obama's *Audacity of Hope* should suffice.
Over 25 points: They are evil racists. Dock their pocket money immediately

12

What can we learn from celebrity fathers?

> *"You need a license to buy a dog or to drive a car, but any f**ker can be a father."*
> **~ Keanu Reeves, Parenthood**

> *"My mum told me the best time to ask my dad for anything was during sex. Not the best advice I'd ever been given. I burst in through the bedroom door saying 'Can I have a new bike?'. He was very upset. His secretary was surprisingly nice about it. I got the bike."*
> **~ Jimmy Carr**

Famous people are the people we could be if only a few more people knew about us. They are special, and all of them make great parents, even the ones who don't.

After all, you can't prick the national consciousness by sitting on your arse watching famous people on TV all day. Unlike you, they've actually *achieved* something in their lives.

So who better to look to for guidance on being a father?

Picking just a few examples wasn't easy with so many to choose from, so here are fifteen from whom we can all learn to be better at raising our children.

In the interests of fairness and balance, I've also dug out the fifteen worst celebrity fathers of all time.

10 best ever celebrity fathers
1. Shane Warne
All children need a father to look up to and respect, someone to go to for sensible advice and counseling when life throws you a googlie. Warney's kids could certainly rely on their dad for all of those… as long as the advice they needed was about spin bowling or hair restoration. On those, Shane has endless anecdotes and hilarious stories to share. If, however, they need practical support from a responsible parent, they'd be better off trying their hot, new stepmum.

What we can learn: Leg spin is all about turning the ball from the legside of a right-handed batsman to the off-side, so your best bet is to make sure the top joints of your index and middle fingers are along the seam so that the ball is nestled between your bent third finger and your thumb. As you let go, flick your wrist so the palm finishes facing downwards and straighten the fingers to allow the third finger to twist the ball anti-clockwise.

2. Mel Gibson
Being a good Catholic, Mel has about thirty children (give or take twenty-two) and has devoted his life to being a great role model. Young people today need a father figure who can teach them how to deal with life's little hiccups – things like traffic cops, ex-wives, gays, AA meetings and the nation of Israel. Also, condoms are a sin against God's will*

What he can teach us: That if one of our teenage daughters goes out looking like 'that', she'll be raped by a pack of, er, well, anyway, it won't be pleasant.

3. John Deaves
This loving dad is best known for having a daughter…with his own daughter. The proud Australian demonstrates admirably that love for

---

* Though He might have made an exception the night Mel's parents conceived him.

our children doesn't end when they leave home. It just gets more... well, more illegal. Poor John had to put up with interfering do-gooders waffling on about genetic abnormalities due to incest. Pah!

What he can teach us: That simultaneously being your own daughter's father and grandfather only makes you more 'special'. And being your own father-in-law means there's one less person to be upset with you.

4. Kim Jung III

As fathers, our primary role is to provide for our children. We need to feed and clothe them, protect them from danger and make sure we have a militaristic communist nation to bequeath them when we're gone.

In refreshing contrast to those modern day parents who fritter away their kids' inheritance on luxuries like old people's homes and food, Kim even managed to store up a few nukes for his heir, Kim Jong Un to play with.

What he can teach us: That everyone being equal is great as long as you personally are more equal than the rest of the population. Also, smocks are flattering to the fuller-figured gentleman.

5. Julian Assange

The WikiLeaks founder is a good example of effective parenting by proxy. OK, so he's not exactly there for his teenage son every *single* day, but at least the boy can read about his dad's heroic exploits and aspire to similar glory, if not similar hair.

What he can teach us: How to hack the school computer to improve our grades.

6. Arnold Schwarzenegger

When parents employ a nanny, it can sometimes be hard for her to feel a part of the family. Our favourite Austrian bodybuilder-turned-actor-turned-politician-turned actor had a unique and sensible solution to this problem: starting a family with her. Voila! His kids get a new sibling and the nanny doesn't feel marginalized. Everyone's a winner. Apart from Mrs Governator, and arguably Arnie who, in fact, lost his family in the process.

What he can teach us: The importance of learning basic mathematics. If he'd done so maybe he wouldn't have nearly bankrupted the world's eighth largest economy.

7. Tiger Woods

While Arnie's kids faced the shame and embarrassment of his major faux pas*, Tiger's little cubs were too young to realise their dad had become better known for driving over fire hydrants and shagging models than for his abilities on the fairways. The moral being, that if you are going to turn from a Tiger into a cheater, at least do it early.

What he can teach us: While you're playing around, swinging your shaft, and ending up in the wrong hole can be expensive. Also, like a seal, you risk being clubbed to death by a Norwegian.

8. Michael Jackson

Too many fathers today let their kids wander around in public without protective blankets over their heads. And few can be arsed to actively demonstrate to a baby the potential perils of dangling off a balcony. Despite the fact that, when it came to child safety, Jacko was whiter than white, some parents still didn't like to leave him in charge of their kids, which was a terrible shame.

What he can teach us: How it's perfectly possible to have three healthy kids without resorting to any of that unseemly 'sex' business.

9. Ozzy Osbourne

If there's one thing kids love it's when one or both their parents are seen as 'different' or 'weird'. No youngster has ever been bullied

---

* No, not The Expendables 2

in the playground because their dad did something in public that was in any way embarrassing... like biting the head off a live bat or, worse, speaking in a thick Birmingham accent.

No one can doubt that Ozzy loves his kids to bits – even when he can't quite remember who they are, or who he is. And, as they grew, if ever there was a time one of them went off the rails, he would leapt into action and get the MTV film crew round to record the moment for millions of people to watch.

What he can teach us: That if one of our children is going through a tough patch, and facing a crisis, then Ozzy's track *Suicide Solution* should cheer them up no end. And just because two US teens shot themselves after listening to it, doesn't necessarily mean yours will.

10. Hulk Hogan

Some self-important psychologist may claim that if a teenage girl's dad has an affair with her best friend, it would be the most embarrassing and humiliating experience of her life.

Not even close! Hulk's daughter, Brooke, might have felt that at the time, but far worse was to follow when her then 59-year-old pops' sex tape was leaked showing him and his handlebar moustache trying a few sexy holds with the ex wife of someone called Bubba The Love Sponge.

What he can teach us: That if taking bucket loads of steroids makes your kids proud, then what's the harm? Nothing! Apart from brain damage, violent mood swings, reduced sex drive, kidney failure, depression, fatigue, testicle shrinkage, insomnia, prostate cancer, infertility and the growth of breasts.

We've examined the very best in fatherhood, so it's only right that we look at the polar opposite. Can it ever be the case that a well-known public figure is actually a bad father?

The answer may shock you. Probably it won't though as it's 'yes'. In fact history is littered with men who give us great fathers a bad name. Crucially, we can learn just as much from their mistakes as we did from the textbook behaviour we've just looked at.

12 worst ever celebrity dads

1. Lot

A hero of both The Bible and the Qur'an, Lot was a drunkard who made both his daughters pregnant after first offering them to an angry mob of townsfolk as prostitutes when they were still virgins. His wife would probably have been appalled had she not just turned into a pillar of salt. And remember Lot was the one God _spared_ from Sodom and Gomorrah.

2. Cronos

Who he? Well, you should have heard of him as he was once the ruler of the world, at least the Ancient Greeks thought so. He was also the father of several gods and goddesses, and came to power after he had castrated his own father. He was then warned that one of his children would one day depose him, so Cronos did what any self-respecting father would have done: he ate all his kids. His wife wasn't best pleased, so the next time she was about to give birth, she gave him a stone wrapped in swaddling clothes to swallow while she sneaked off to give birth to Zeus. Then, when her waters broke while delivering Poseidon, she handed him a horse to snack on instead. The old boy never suspected a thing.

3. Peter the Great

Great by name, but not great by his parenting skills. Having single-handedly turned his son, Alexis, into an alcoholic, Pete told him he was going to 'cut you off like a gangrened limb'. When that didn't work, he had his son tortured and killed. He had thirteen other kids, so figured he'd get over it.

4. Herod the Great

Another boastfully named man, but another disastrous dad. Herod executed two of his sons for attempted parricide. When they'd had the chance to look the word up, they realised he was accusing them of trying to kill their parents*. And not for them a noble hanging or beheading – both were strangled to death.

However, Herod is best remembered for killing lots of other little kiddies in Bethlehem in his search for the baby Jesus. All of which is a bit unfair, as the old guy had actually died a couple of years earlier.

5. Bing Crosby

Christmases in the Crosby home weren't so much 'white' as 'shite', Bing being a notoriously cruel father who pushed two of his kids to shoot themselves in the head and the third to write a tell-all book about their hellish childhood. In his defence, he was a good golfer and made pipe smoking cool.

6. Brutus

Like Cronos before him, Brutus was brutal when it came to brutalising and killing his own sons. Admittedly he didn't eat many of them**, but makes the list of shame because he resorted to murder whenever he suspected them of treason. So, depending on your perspective, he was either impressively patriotic for putting his country first, or an unimpressive father for siring so many traitors.

7. Darth Vader

If destroying your daughter's favourite planet wasn't enough, Darth then decided to teach his son, Luke a lesson by cutting off his hand, ending any ambition he might have had to play jazz guitar. His parenting style is probably best described as 'a bit evil'.

* The Latin root should have made this obvious to them
** Or so he claims

8. Marvin Gay Sr

Ok, so he shot his famous son dead after a little tiff, but who hasn't been driven crazy by their kids? Ironically he used the Smith & Wesson that his son had given him to use to protect himself. Despite shooting the singer twice at point blank range, he was only charged with voluntary manslaughter and put on probation for five years. Marvin Sr was also probably also a bit peeved that his son had added an 'e' to the end of his surname.

9. Ivan the Terrible

Ivan's family should have taken the hint that anyone with the moniker 'The Terrible' probably isn't going to be a touchy feely dad. And ruling Russian in the Sixteen Century only made him more tetchy. Once, when he thought his pregnant daughter-in-law was dressed too immodestly, he beat her so badly she miscarried. When Ivan's son remonstrated, Ivan hit him on the head with a staff and killed him, which taught him never to argue back with Dad.

10. King Laius

Having been warned by several Greek prophesies not to have any kids because they would end up killing him and marrying his widow, randy old Laius couldn't resist and, hey presto, he was slain by his son, Oedipus who then married his own mother. One of Oedipus' motives might have been revenge for the fact that his name translates as 'swollen foot'.

Another example of his limited fatherhood skills was when he offered to teach another king's son how to ride a chariot, and then raped him.

11. Ryan O'Neill

Anyone who makes a pass his own daughter at her mother's funeral isn't going to be shortlisted for Father of the Year. And, in fairness, he didn't realise it was Tatum: "I had just put the casket in the hearse and I was watching it drive away when a beautiful blonde woman comes up and embraces me," he told Vanity Fair. "I said to her, 'You have a drink on you? You have a car?' She said, 'Daddy, it's me, Tatum!' I was just trying to be funny with a strange Swedish woman, and it's my daughter. It's so sick."

All four of Ryan's kids have been in rehab, while his eldest son was jailed for heroin abuse. When asked why he was such a terrible dad, Ryan answered: 'I wasn't trained'.

12. Jack Torrance, The Shining

Chasing your son through a maze armed with an axe in midwinter is never a sensible plan, especially if you're not wearing a warm coat. Poor old Jack, having been driven to the brink of insanity by his unreasonable family while he did his best to be a decent caretaker at the Overlook Hotel, needed an outlet to his frustrations. And trying to bash his wife's brains in with a baseball bat hadn't done the trick. All work and no play had made Jack a seriously deranged boy and not the greatest role model for his lad.

13

All your Questions Answered

*Guys may come and guys may go, but daddy's always daddy...
well, at least until he jumps a freight train.*
~ *Al Bundy, Married With Children*

"My dad always used to say 'fight fire with fire', which s probably why he was thrown out of the fire brigade."
~ *Harry Hill*

My little boy's pet rabbit, Bernard, died suddenly last night, and I've no idea what to tell him. He'll be devastated.
Jamie, 32, Burnley

The death of a pet can be very upsetting for a child. Often it is the first time they will have felt grief. Firstly reassure them that what they are going through will prepare them for when their grandparents die followed eventually by you and their mum. Then they'll see that losing a pet that couldn't even fetch a stick, is not worth losing sleep over.

My fifteen-year-old daughter wants her boyfriend to come for a sleepover. She says there will be no funny business, but I'm really worried as I suspect he's a randy goat beneath his mature exterior.
Maurice, 48, Haslemere

There comes a point when, as a parent, you need to show your teenager that you trust them to take responsibility and do the right thing. When they realise that their dad is letting them demonstrate their maturity, they won't want to let you down. Unfortunately for you, that time has not yet come. In this instance, let her know that the boy is welcome to stay, but that you will be sleeping on an airbed between them armed with an assault rifle.

My son, Emile, is getting in with a bad crowd. Many of his friends hang out on street corners drinking and smoking, and I know at least one of them steals money to buy hard drugs; and another is already sleeping with his girlfriend. How can I stop him throwing his life away before he's even six?
    Alistair, 41, Ipswich
    This one's easy - your boy isn't watching enough TV. If he was then he'd learn that bad people rarely triumph, and that anti-social behaviour leads to tough consequences. For example, in Teletubbies, when Noo Noo made too much tubby toast, he had to face up to his actions and calm down a very agitated Dipsy. And in Scooby Doo, when old Mr Bobbins, the fairground worker tried to scare off kids by dressing up as a ghoul, he was sent down for thirty years without the prospect of parole. Not even the sight of Shaggy hilariously tripping over a sandwich at the end could cheer him up.

My wife is pregnant with our first child, and I'm worried that it's going to be a boy and I'll be a terrible role model. I know nothing about fixing car engines, or sports, or DIY. Will he think less of me?
    David, 28, Dartmouth
    Yes. Next question. Okay, well, you might be able to salvage something here, by brainwashing him from an early age to take an interest in things that you *do* know about. Then, he'll be the proudest boy in the world because whatever he talks about, his dad knows all about it. The only slight issue may be when he gets to school and finds not all his classmates have a specialized interest in the history of yogurt production, PG Wodehouse or brass rubbing.

Wait a minute, as far as I know there's only one Maurice in Haslemere, and my son, Charlie is dating his daughter. Let me tell you, matey, that my son is no goat and would *never* sleep with your daughter (unlike the rest of the town's teenage boys, so I'm told). And anyway, my wife and I suspect Charlie is gay, so if you do sleep next to him excuse his wandering hands.
Marcus, 45, Haslemere

The gentleman in Burnley whose son's rabbit died is beneath contempt. There are millions of rabbits running wild in this country, largely thanks to people like him encouraging kids to own them as pets. When my wife bought one for our daughter, I injected it with myxomatosis there and then. That taught them. And when I'm allowed back in the family home, I'm thinking of doing the same to the Labradoodle before it goes rogue.
Max, 55, St Ives

I work digging ditches alongside the A303 in Somerset and my wife is a part time dinner lady. If one of our eleven kids decides they want to go to uni, should I sell my yacht or the ski lodge to pay for it?
Craig, 50, Bridgwater

It's a sad fact that our younger generation grows up thinking that the world owes them a living. They assume that you will pay for their trumpet lessons, soccer coaching, ballet shoes and diabetes medication. And that you should work all hours to fund them going to some la-di-da college to study a Mickey Mouse subject like sociology, food science or law. Hammer into all of them from an early age, that if they want to be like their old man, they don't need to waste valuable time 'learning things'.

Oh, so it's my daughter who's the problem is it, Marcus? Well let me make one thing clear – the only people my daughter has slept with were vetted by me personally.
Maurice, 48, Haslemere

Does anyone know how to strip the carburetor in a Nissan Primera?
    Tim, 29, Kettering

I'm sure some of us do, but that's not strictly a question about fatherhood, is it now?

My granddaughter told me the funniest story. It was about a hosepipe called Harold, and...
    Stan, 64, Tadcaster

I'm going to have to stop you there, Stan, and refer you to the next book in this series, *Muddle Your Way Through Being a Grandparent*. It will contain everything you will ever need to know.

Look, I'm not saying nothing, but if the bloke with the rabbit had got 'imself a Cashmere Lop, it probably would have lived a bit longer. If you get a Netherlands Dwarf, it's your own bleedin' look out if it conks out. Them's only good for eatin'.
    Andy, 29, Tottenham

I'm an atheist and my wife is an agnostic. We keep arguing about what religion not to bring out children up in. Can you help?
    George, 30, Carlisle

Not really, but if you refer to the letter above, you can at least be better informed when buying a rabbit.

My wife and I have decided to separate after nineteen years of marriage. It feels like my life has fallen apart and I wonder if it really is worth going on living. We were only blessed with one child, Terrence, who's eleven, and is already so traumatized that all he wants to do is spend time with his pets. How can I reach out to him?
    Manny, 43, Royal Tunbridge Wells

There are so many things that need to be said, yet so little space. First things first – if his pet is a rabbit, is it a Netherlands Dwarf or a Cashmere Lop?

I'm sorry, I didn't have my spectacles on me. Could you remind me of the title of the publication I need to purchase? It sounds marvelous. Only yesterday, my grandson, Levi said the funniest...
(this letter has been abridged)
Stan, 64, Tadcaster
Sure, Stan. It's *Muddle Your Way Through Being a Grandparent*. In literary circles, it's already being touted as 'prime landfill'.

Oh, so he's gay, is he? That old trick. If I had five cents for every young lad who has slept beside me in my daughter's bedroom and pretended to be gay, I'd be a very rich man indeed.
Marcus, 45, Haslemere

I agreed to teach my daughter to drive, but now we're six miles out of town on the A43, and I've just realised that I can't drive either. Can anyone pick us up? We're in an ice cream van.
Kevin, 39, Corby

My son, Jake is the shortest in his class. He also has a wizened left hand and is cross-eyed. To try to make him feel better I bought him a sea captain's hat, and an eye patch, but he refuses to wear them.
Simon, 34, Great Yarmouth
Children are like slaughterhouses – they don't want you to see what's happening on the inside (and they often pollute local water systems). Jake has put up with a lot in his short life, so you'll need to handle this one carefully. If he's self-conscious about his hand, you could give him one of those costume party plastic hooks to hold to disguise it; and how about a pair of knee-high pirate boots with a built up sole. He'll soon start fitting in.

Kev, if you're six miles out of Corby, then you're just down the road from me. If I can strip this bloody carburetor then I can

give you a lift. Any chance of some fudge choc chip when I get there?
   Tim, 29, Kettering

I also have a son called Derek, if that helps, but unfortunately he hasn't told me any funny stories. Mainly because he's been in a permanent vegetative state since 1998. I remember the year because Celine Dion sang that Titanic song. He'd always hated her so he probably wanted us to turn it off. My granddaughter, however, well she started talking to hosepipes when...
   (this letter has been abridged)
   Stan, 64, Tadcaster

As a Scientologist, I want my kids to understand that Xenu brought his peoples to Earth seventy five million years ago in VC-8 planes, stacked them all around volcanoes and used hydrogen bombs to kill everyone, but that their essence still remains in the form of evil spirits and therefore no women should use pain relief during childbirth. Now I've been banned from helping out at my son's religious studies class.
   Bob, 44, Margate
   So-called teachers can adopt an almost fascist obsession with what can loosely be termed 'facts'. Instead of opening their minds to other theories of the universe, they are actively brainwashing our kids into blindly accepting questionable doctrines like science, nature, maths and history. This narrow-mindedness has the sinister side effect – it calls religion into question. You and I know The Bible is true because Jesus told us it was, and He wouldn't lie. And nor would L Ron Hubbard because he had nothing to gain by converting rich people to his cause and making them give him all their money, did he? Take your son out of school before it's too late.

"Any chance of a fudge choc chip when I get there". Clearly a reference to my Charlie. Shame on you people. He doesn't hang

around ice cream vans offering sexual favours, you know. Not anymore.
Marcus, 45, Haslemere

Am I a bad dad because I told my three-year-old twins that Santa isn't real?
Dan, 25, Bootle

Did you not even read the last but one answer? Of course you are. By telling them the 'truth', you are setting a very dangerous precedent. As they are so young, there is still time to convince them that you were heavily drunk when you blurted out an ugly lie about Father Christmas.

I have a better suggestion for the dad who dressed his freaky little boy up as a pirate. When my son had his hair shaved off accidentally, I put a bandanna on him, found some Ray Bans, a stick-on moustache and an ammunition belt, and hey presto, with a little shoe polish on his face, he made a great Somali pirate.
JT, 33, Armagh

I've got just one word for Dan in Bootle: very poor form. Santa Claus is as much a part of Christmas as the baby Jesus and Brussels sprouts. I will not be telling my kids that he isn't real as I want the magic to remain for as long as possible. I also haven't told my grandchildren or great grandchildren either for that matter.
Ted, 85, Clapham

If there were more parents like you, Ted, the world would be a better place. And if any kids are reading this, ignore what Ted says about Father Christmas not being real, he's obviously a confused old person in need of his meds.

I've never owned a rabbit. Can I still ask a question?
Eddie, 37, Welwyn Garden City
Okay, as long as it isn't about fudge choc chip.

I've been driving up and down the A43 for an hour now, and I can't see you, Kev. Have you got the jingly jangly music playing?
   Tim, 29, Kettering

Damn. Oh, well in that case I suppose I'll have to ask another, slightly more helpful parenting book.
   Eddie, 37, Welwyn Garden City

My son is refusing to go to school because he gets teased by the children just because he has a ponytail. He stays up in his bedroom crying and pretending to be sick. It's been a week now, and I don't know what to do. If he doesn't go back soon, they'll find another head teacher to replace him.
   Albert, 65, Loughborough

If this book has taught you nothing else (and let's face it, that's a very real possibility), you should at least have realised that you don't stop worrying about your children when the become adults. If a kid gets upset, you can simply tell them that everything will be okay and they will believe you. Adults are more savvy. Perhaps if you took him to school yourself and held his hand in the playground, he might regain some of his confidence.

Hee hee! I had a rabbit once, and once he was fully dressed, he…
   Stan, 64, Tadcaster
   (this letter has been abridged)

I'm probably being paranoid, but I'm worried that my daughter is sniffing glue. She's seventeen and the other day I caught her

with a tube of No More Nails stuck to her left nostril. The following evening it was a Pritt Stick and then yesterday I found a stash of industrial glue in her bottom drawer. Not only that, I checked her Internet history and found she'd searched for 'best glues to sniff' and 'how to get high on glue'. Her complexion is all pale and sallow and judging by the series of men who visit her bedroom every day, she's turning tricks to feed her habit. Am I worrying unnecessarily?
  Justin, 42, Glasgow

I'm sure there isn't a father alive who hasn't had similar concerns. It's in our genes to protect our kin, so sometimes we interpret perfectly innocent things as somehow sinister or worrying. There's every chance she's not about to die of respiratory failure.

Will you be putting an index in the book, Paul, so that I know where to find things?
  Miles, 35, Newcastle

No.

Conclusion

"I'm cool dad, that's my thang. I'm hip, I surf the web, I text. LOL: laugh out loud, OMG: oh my god, WTF: why the face."

"I always felt bad for people with emotionally distant fathers; it turns out I'm one of them. It's a miracle I didn't end up a stripper.
~ Phil Dunphy, Modern Family

Becoming a father is a lot like climbing a tree. Before you start it can seem daunting, but if you take one branch at a time, then your view changes and you feel more secure. You try each foothold and then trust your instinct as to whether it'll support your weight. Then, er well, you get comfy and the branches turn to sticks and…

Okay, maybe that metaphor doesn't really work. Try viewing being a dad as attempting to run through a minefield while snipers try to take you out and US drones rain down from the sky as you run. If you get to the other side without having your limbs blown off then you've succeeded. And if instead you end up with body parts splattered over the battlefield, you have at least learnt a valuable lesson.

I hope that's somehow reassuring.

Whatever fatherhood is, it isn't like a box of chocolates because you know exactly what you're going to get*.

What I hope this book has made you realise is that you don't need a book like this to trick people into thinking you're a great dad. Curiously I chose not to put that line on the back cover blurb. Fatherhood is all about expecting the unexpected, like stepping on a thick-looking

* So maybe more like a bag of Maltesers, except with hard centres that are not at all easy to chew.

branch, but being ready for it to be rotten, snap off and leave you plummeting to your death*.

Your kids will learn just as much from your mistakes as from your successes. After all, they are learning to be kids at the same time.

Above all, starting a family is the most exciting thing that will ever happen to you. You get to pass on your genes to future generations and, who knows maybe one of your descendents will become prime minister, be a captain of industry, a noted philanthropist or join a boy band.

And their achievements will, in part, be because of what they learnt from you. And possibly some exceptional DNA from your wife's side of the family.

If you bought this book to help you decide whether or not to have children, then I think we can both agree there is only one answer. I won't tell you what it is because that would be wrong. You need to feel it in your heart and soul, have a knot in your gut that instinctively tells you the answer and come to the right choice given everything you've earned in your life both from your parents and these pages. Oh all right, it's 'yes'. But you knew that.

I wish you well, and, more importantly, I wish your children the best of luck as they blossom into little saplings of their own, nervously pushing their shoots up through the forest floor, looking for shards of sunlight, nutrients in the soil and hoping one day to become the sturdy oak tree that is you.

Nah, the tree metaphor is still shit.

* Hmm, that's still a terrible comparison. Remind me to think of something else.

Appendix
Fatherhood by numbers

34
Average age of a first time married dad in the UK

1910
Year of the very first Father's Day, held in Spokane, Arkansas. It was the idea of Sonara Louse Smart, who lobbied her local church to celebrate it in honour of her widowed father who had raised six kids. Greetings card manufacturers the world over rejoiced.

1988
Year of biggest surge in birth rate in New Zealand's history…nine months after they won the inaugural Rugby World Cup.

96
Age of oldest man ever to father a child, Ramajit Raghav from Haryana, north of Delhi. The randy bugger beat his own record as he had another son two ears earlier with his sprightly fifty-two-year-old wife. The labourer credits his fertitilty to an alcohol-free lifestyle and regular afternoon naps.

11
Age of Sean Stewart, from Bedford, England, when he knocked up his fifteen-year-old next door neighbour. Nine months later, only a

month after his twelveth birthday, he was given a day off school for the birth of his son, Ben. Sadly the couple split up and later Sean was sent to prison for theft.

300
Maximum number of offspring a male seahorse can give birth to after incubating the eggs for a month. The female sticks a tube in her mate and impregnates him with her egg. Then, the same day he pops them all out, he goes back to the same partner and the cycle begins again. Sucker.

727
Weight in kilos of the biggest ever grizzly bear, the species that arguably make nature's worst dads. Adult bears routinely kill and even eat their young if they invade their territory. One theory is that they do this so that the female bears are freed up to be impregnated again.

112,000,000
Google hits for 'dad'. 'Mum' by comparison gets four million more.

Six
Number of years Rolling Stone Keith Richards kept his father's ashes in an urn before he mixed some of them with cocaine and snorted it. The rest was scattered round an oak tree.

634
Weight in kilos of the heaviest dad in history, Jon Brower Minnoch from Washington State, USA. He somehow managed to have two kids with his 50kg wife before dying aged forty-one. Fertility specialists have said it 'unlikely' that they used the missionary position.

10
Number of sons of boxing champ George Forman who were all also called George. His one daughter was named Georgetta.

21:15

Verse of Exodus in the Old Testament that states that any child who strikes their dad should be put to death. The Bible also records how God killed forty-two children because some of them had been taking the piss out of a bald man (2 Kings 2:23-24.) Not to be outdone, Jesus also advocates murdering children if they curse their parents (Matthew 15: 4-7). To be fair, this was a few years before the naughty step was invented.

800

Children estimated to have been fathered by the last Sharifian Emperor of Morocco, the most prolific dad in history. He had over five hundred wives, so as never short of odd jobs to do round the house.

8

Hours a night that Rhianna's dad, Ronald, made her sit outside their home in Bridgetown, Barbados as a child looking for UFOs. She never saw one.

73

Number of entrants in Australia's Most Mentally Sexy Dad 2011 competition, run by reservoirdad.com. Each of the five finalists won a Dyson animal vacuum cleaner.

1207

Years before Christ was born that the earliest ever incidence of a boy murdering his father was recorded. Asher-nadin-apli was the son of the king of Assyria (modern day Iraq), Tukulti-Ninurta I and has his eyes on the throne soon after his dad captured the city of Babylon.

1 in 200

People in the world who are direct descendents of 13th century Mongolian leader Genghis Khan, according to geneticists. That's sixteen million of us.

100

Hours of community service given to forty-seven-year-old Tuan Huynh, who abandoned his sixteen-year-old daughter on a street corner because she got poor grades in calculus. He made her to pack some clothes and a blanket and then drive her fifteen miles to an intersection in Cheltenham, Pennsylvania, dumped her by the roadside and warned her not to tell the cops who she was. Firm, but fair.

64

Consecutive days a male emperor penguin balances its egg on its feet to prevent it freezing in the cruel Antarctic winter. By the time the egg hatches, the dad will have gone without food for 115 days and lost half its body weight. .

107

Number of times the three letters 'dad' appear in this book. Except now, it's 108.

Coming soon!

MUDDLE YOUR WAY THROUGH BEING A GRANDPARENT
by Paul Merrill

As if your kids hadn't done enough damage - now they've gone and made you a grandparent. And at your age! Well don't panic! Yet. This book will arm you with the essential cheats and tricks the so-called experts don't dare tell you.

Covering everything from believable excuses to get out of babysitting and how to tell your daughter she's a hopeless mum to ways not to have your house destroyed, how to avoid being dumped in a home and a handy guide to interpreting teen speak that's so lol, you'll rofl.

Aimed at today's modern generation of grandparents who refuse to be treated as bufuddled old dears, this award-worthy book will take you through a hilarious series scientifically questionable quizzes, flowcharts, comedy tips, role playing exercises, celebrity advice and checklists.

Learn coping strategies for a daughter-in-law from hell, the perils of the granny flat and discover if you're already losing your memory.

Find out:

- What to do if your grandchild is ugly
- Which swear words are appropriate for oldies
- How to steer your daughter away from choosing ridiculous names
- Ways to make your grandkids think you're a 'funky crumbly'
- How to invent a more interesting family tree
- What happens when grannies go evil
- Ideas for amusing last words
- Whether your grandson is an emo, a nerd or a neek.
- Simple ways to make your war stories more exciting
- What presents they might not completely hate

Plus! Find out if you're already losing your memory.

Of course you could read a normal book on grandparenting full of 'useful advice', nice, fluffy ways to bond with your grandchild and Oprah-inspired tips on modern child rearing. Yes, it might make you a better grandparent.

But at what cost?

Your children have an agenda here, and you need to understand what it is. Even now, they are plotting ways to exploit your energy, money and digestive biscuits.

With this book, the fight back begins…

Follow Paul @paulmerrill68

Printed in Great Britain
by Amazon.co.uk, Ltd.,
Marston Gate.